KINGDOMGARTEN
KIDS

KINGDOMGARTEN
KIDS

Becoming "As" a Little Child

BOB MCCLAIN

Kravitz & Sons
INNOVATORS IN PUBLISHING, MARKETING AND ADVERTISING

Kravitz and Sons LLC
1301 Farmville Blvd, Suite 104
Greenville, NC 27834

Published by Kravitz and Sons LLC.

ISBN: 979-8-89639-054-1 (sc)
ISBN: 979-8-89639-053-4 (e)

Library of Congress Control Number: 2024927529

Table of Contents

Dedication

This book is dedicated to all the great men and women who dared to look beyond the regions of church doctrines and dogmas and embrace the glorious majesty of God's unshakeable kingdom.

To the men and women who loved all people regardless of color, creed, denomination, or doctrine. To the unsung heroes, people whose names are not found in encyclopedias, or on the internet, but will forever be remembered and cherished in the hearts and lives of those they touched in this life.

These men and women made the generational transfer of godly inheritance that can only be made by those who see and enter God's glorious kingdom.

Foreword

From time to time I am asked to forward a book or write a "blurp" for some related ministry friend or associate. Most often these requests are made with the idea that I probably already know something about the theme or point being made in the manuscript. My willingness to oblige is usually based on my care for the writer as much as for what they have written.

Since my relationship with Bob McClain has for years been a precious personal treasure and knowing without doubt the heart and character of this profoundly consistent man of God, I agreed to forward his book only a cursory glimpse at the double spaced pages laying on my desk.

I smiled when I read the "cute" title Kindomgarten Kids thinking to myself that the words written on the following pages were no doubt driven by Bob's years as a superb educator coupled with his gentle approach to pasturing. While this assumption was not in any way incorrect, what I did not anticipate was the powerful way in which he so skillfully managed to subtly clothe the deepest issues of Kingdom living in the garments of childlike simplicity.

As I turned page after page, I found myself immersed in an ocean of thought pulled by the tides of words and acknowledged reality. This book was making me think and its message commanded me to deal again with long neglected issues.

"Why do so many Christians claim abundant life and live with unbelievable stress?" "Why do we claim to love unconditionally and live with anger and unforgiveness?" These and another thousand thoughts passed through my mind while I conceited that Bob McClain had coaxed me into a sandbox and then managed to bulldoze into mountains of debris present in my spirit.

After reading Kingdomgarten Kids now for a second time, I am in a state of spiritual reflection. The Apostle Paul was correct. We have been "corrupted from the simplicity that is in Christ." There are fundamental reasons why the greater percentage of people converted to Christ are won by those who have been saved six months or less. The fruit of the Spirit is to most of us an ideal to be reached but rarely ever achieved, while the works of the flesh are too many Christians considered to be unavoidable weaknesses which never expected to be conquered.

Bob McClain in this powerful presentation clearly defines the Kingdom of God as a lifestyle...not a message. The Kingdom is within us...not around us. The power of the Gospel of the Kingdom is in its simplicity not its profundity.

This is Christianity 101. It is the formula for achieving what the New Testament states should be our final position in Christian maturity... "in malice be ye children but in understanding be ye men." In many cases it seems we have achieved a degree in doctrine and failed the course on perfecting fruit.

Every Christian should read Kingdomgarten Kids once and weep. Then we should read it again and smile. The truth contained in this book could set us free and could very well turn our... "sorrow into joy."

Respectfully,
Dr. Mark Hanby

Introduction

It was said of Robert Fulghum that he managed to keep his sense of childlike wonder well preserved. Fulghum, for those not familiar, wrote a number one bestseller entitled, All I needed to know I learned in Kindergarten. Wisdom, according to Fulghum, was not on the top of the graduate school mountain, but was right there in the sand pile at Sunday school. Here are the things that he says he learned:

Share everything
Play fair
Don't hit people
Put things back where you found them
Clean up your own mess
Don't take things that aren't yours
Say you're sorry when you hurt somebody
Wash your hands before you eat
Flush
Warm cookies and cold milk are good for you
Live a well-balanced life, learn some and think some and draw
    and paint and sing and dance and work every day some
Take a nap every afternoon
When you go out into the world, watch out for traffic, hold
    hands,
And stick together
Be aware of wonder

I have chosen these excerpts from Mr. Fulghum's book to begin the introduction to my book because I believe that the things that he says he learned in kindergarten are the things that all people should learn and treasure for life. Growing older is a reality of life, but growing older and being mean, hateful, and unfulfilled is not very desirable. I've been a Christian since 1980 and some of the unhappiest and meanest people I've ever met I met them right in church. I do not say this with disdain but I say it because it's true.

Christians often miss the spiritual meaning of things that lie within the simple things in life because we're always looking for something deep and powerful. We become wise in our own eyes and forget that God purposely chooses the foolish things of this world to confound the wise (1 Corinthians 1:27). Whenever Jesus taught about the Kingdom of God He would always use things that existed in the natural world to illustrate His lessons, or parables. He used trees, seeds, farmers, fishing nets, coins, sheep, and even children to get people to embrace the Kingdom.

In Matthew 18:3, Jesus said that unless we got converted and become as little children, we would not enter the Kingdom of heaven. So it's possible for people to be church members but totally ignorant of God's glorious kingdom. The apostle Paul adds support to what Jesus said when he told the Corinthian church to be like children when it comes to malice, but like men when it comes to understanding (1 Corinthians 14:20). Children do indeed have problems and disagreements with one another but they usually don't last very long. It's possible for us to grow older and become spiritually mature, and at the same time retain the heart and spirit of a small child. This may be the reason why the bible often refers to us as "children".

What I hope to do in writing this book is to remind people, especially Christians, of how children behave, and to remember the simple lessons we learned way back in kindergarten, whether it was church school or grade school. Christians are fussing and fighting all the time nowadays over issues that prevent them from being productive in their lives because they're locked into a churchy–church mentality. If Christians become kingdomgarten kids they will live much longer and will enjoy better health.

The woman with the issue of blood in Luke chapter 5 was unproductive for twelve years of her life. She was bleeding on the inside. A woman who's trying to get pregnant and have a child longs for the time when her monthly cycle stops flowing. Millions of people are dying today because they refuse to become as little children and touch the hem of Jesus' garment (let go of pride). People are fighting over who's the greatest, who's church is bigger, the name of their church, whose name is used in baptism, positions, titles, and what someone did to them over twenty years ago mainly because they refuse to become as little children. People are spiritually bleeding to death. They're also angry and can't explain why. I've never seen so many angry people in my life.

God actually allows us to be angry for an allotted time, but I'm afraid that many people have become angry and stayed angry too long. I believe that God grants believers a "grace period for anger and grief. Maybe this is where creditors got the idea of giving borrowers a grace period for paying bills. The bill is due on the first of the month, but you have until the tenth to pay it without late charges being added. Late charges hurt you in a couple of ways; they will lower your credit score and cause you to have to pay a much higher interest rate when you do get credit, and it's also costing you money you could otherwise keep. Failure to get positive answers to prayers could be the result of bad credit with God.

As sure as you're alive you will have problems with other people, but it's wrong to live year after year with clutter in your heart. I know people who have worked diligently to remove things from their credit report, but the same people profess to be Christians and are not the least bit concerned about the bitterness they have in their hearts toward others. I guess they think God just wipes it off their record after so long a time. Like children, we should forgive each other quickly, and seek to continue growing in wisdom and understanding. God has put us in the midst of people we like as well as people we have issues with. It is God who is in charge and not us. God loves you, but He has no problem with giving you an "early out" from this earthly life if you insist.

All of us need to understand that we're here on this earth for God's glorious purpose, and not just to occupy space. We need to learn how to have fun and stop taking ourselves so serious.

God is all authority and power, and if He had wanted to He could have brought all of us into this world as full-grown adults, but He chose to start us out as infants, and totally dependent upon someone else to care for us. Do you remember what it was like to have to get your diaper changed? What about sitting in the high chair with your mouth open waiting for Mommy to put the baby formula in your mouth? By the way, your diaper smelled really gross. Now the people who loved and cared for us when we were babies didn't mind the fact that we cried, got into stuff, had a stinky diaper, or had to be fed. No, they understood that this was all normal for children. So why is it that as we grow older we forget what it's like to be children, or as my title suggests, "Kingdomgarten kids".

God wants us to understand that we were never supposed to fight over titles, doctrines, greatness, color, positions, or none of the myriad of little foxes that church folk are dying over today. Small children are not concerned with "who's the greatest "discussions. They're more interested in having fun than in having a fuss. When they do fall out with one another it's usually not for long. When we were babies and made a mess, someone else cleaned our mess up for us, but now that we've come of age we must clean our own messes up. We mope and stay depressed far too long about our situations.

My previous occupation as an elementary school teacher and principal afforded me the opportunity to really discover how resilient children were, and how unforgiving some adults can be. Children are like rubber balls- they bounce right back very quickly. Many adults are like sponges- they hold stuff in and won't let go to save their neck. You have to squeeze stuff out of them. As a school principal I had to discipline children who were sent to my office for acting up in class. On occasions I'd have children to return to the class and apologize to the class and also the teacher; however I can remember certain teachers who were not openly ready to receive children back into their classroom after they'd misbehaved. Even though I encouraged teachers not to hold on to the bad choices that children were certain to make, but be willing to give them a fresh start right away, some teachers were bound by pride and unforgiveness.

For most children every day is a new day. For many adults every day is a constant reminder of yesterday's faults, failures, and disappointments. We've forgotten how to forgive, play, have fun, and age gracefully. We're grown now and we've become bible experts and right in our own eyes. Life has not made us better, but more bitter. I've seen people who were so bitter until you could get lock jaw just looking at them. People like this don't need lemons to make lemonade; all they need to do is stir sweet water with their fingers and they'd have enough lemonade to open up a lemonade stand. I can remember one particular teacher who taught under me who was so mean and venomous until if she bit a railroad track, the train would die. Please allow me to exaggerate a bit as I'm trying to stress my point.

It's a disaster to have anyone in a place of authority such as a classroom, a church setting, a giant corporation, or anywhere else, with a mean and hateful spirit. People are having enough problems in their lives nowadays without having to deal with "crabapples" all the time. This is a very serious subject I'm addressing, but I'm humorous by nature, so please hang in there with me. Every church in the world needs a few stand-up comedians who can loosen up those old stiff joints sitting in the pews. You object to comedians in the church because you say that they use cuss words. No, I don't think we should use profane language in the church, but on the other hand neither do I think that we should allow profane faces to come through the door either. If a frowned face was a sin, I know people who would have committed the unpardonable sin.

Speaking of profane language, I started playing golf because someone told me that the game of golf would make a preacher "cuss", well, they were absolutely correct! I'm really glad that I did start playing golf, not because I just wanted to see if I still knew how to cuss, but because I've met so many people I wouldn't have met otherwise. No, I never tell people I meet and play with for the first time that I'm a preacher because that would take all the fun out of playing together. I want people to relax and be themselves, and I know that for most people as soon as they discover they're playing with a preacher- the show begins. I'm not out there playing golf for a show, because if I wanted a show, I'd just hang around religious folk all the time, but I'm out there to "re-create". That's right! I said re-create, and not just recreate. I'm having fun, getting physical exercise, but I'm also being born again, again and again, and again.

The wonderful world of outdoors is the natural world, and the beautiful home of the "green" family. I love coming out to minister to the greens because they minister to me as well. Every time I visit them, I discover another aspect of their personality, and mine as well. They say that golf is not a team sport but it surely does require "teamwork" from every facet of your being Your entire spirit, soul, and body must all work together on the golf course. In my mind I know what to do, but my body doesn't always cooperate. One valuable lesson that I have learned from playing golf is focusing my mind on what I did right.

My spiritual father and friend, Dr. Mark Hanby, has always said that we need to find out what we did right. Anyone who has ever played this game knows that you will hit lots of bad shots, and I have hit a bunch of them; I have however managed to hit the perfect shot at times, and thus I'm back out there trying to see and understand what I did right. Don't waste your time trying to figure out what you did wrong. Your marriage will be better when you study what you did right in a particular situation. As the company CEO, what was it that you did right that caused the employees to get so fired up? What was it that the coach did right that motivated the players so greatly? What was it that the teacher did right that caused so much interest and enthusiasm in the students? What was it that the pastor did right that made everyone stay awake during last Sunday's sermon? The list of wrong things can go on and on, but if we could ever discover that "one" thing that we did right it could change our whole life forever.

You see, golf is not just a foolish game; it's an outdoor lab of fun and experimentation. What if there's a luxurious golf course in heaven? Don't shoot me down so quickly because I have as much proof to support my belief in a heavenly golf course as you do in believing that you have a big old mansion especially built for you up in glory. Maybe if you'd get out some time and walk and see God in all of nature it might help you get rid of your mean and bitter spirit.

Many Christians are mean and evil because they've had the snot beat out of them by their old religious, fundamentalist, stiff-necked parents, and teachers. Their parents and elders are dead and gone but the fruit of their misguided labor is still walking around on God's turf as mixed up and crazy as a deer in headlights. All is not lost however; God still has His hand on you, and has reserved a seat for you in His kingdomgarten class. So stop crying and boohooing for your Mama and get yourself over to your seat and have fun.

We need to rediscover, or discover for the first time, the joy and the freedom of being kingdomgarten kids. Oh come on, I know that the term kingdomgarten is not really in the dictionary. I don't even think it's on the internet. God has given me this term to use in an attempt to show people how much He wants us to learn our one, two, three's and our a,b,c's, and then go out into all the world and be who we are in Him. Just as learning the alphabet and basic number theory are foundational for Kindergarten children, getting a good basic education in church is also crucial for God's kingdomgarten kids. Children who struggle with number theory and alphabet sounds are certain to have difficulty in math and reading, as well as most other subjects.

I aim to show the real reasons why so many Christians today are developmentally delayed, and just can't seem to move on in their life, their job, and their ministry. God means to use all of His people, and not just the ones with lofty titles and positions. The command to go into the entire world was not limited to preachers and the so called anointed men and women of the gospel. Because men have interpreted it to mean this is the reason why so many good men and women died young trying to reach the world all by themselves. God never intended to have a lone ranger, or one-man ministry. He wants to get the worldly mindset, the anti-christed way of thinking, out of His people and then sow us into the entire world, the terra firma, so that His mighty kingdom will cover the earth as the waters cover the seas.

If you still remember, and I'm sure you do, how to count to ten and say your abc's, after all these years, then why has it become so hard for you to practice the basics of the spiritual principles taught to us in church? The basics are not the end of everything; they're just the beginning, and a very necessary beginning, of all you'll ever accomplish in life. All the stuff that church leaders fight over today is basic to Christianity. Whose name you were baptized in is basic. How Christians dress is basic. Repentance and faith are basic. Speaking in tongues, laying on hands, spiritual gifts, tithing, resurrection of the dead, eternal judgment, and the return of Jesus are all basic tenets of the church. These are things that a new saint should know less than two years of being converted. Why are we talking to people about these things every week that have been in the church over twenty years? Well, think about it like this, your little precious five year old that you just dropped off at school for her first day of kindergarten is in serious trouble because her teacher doesn't know her abs's or her 1, 2, 3's. No, I was just kidding. No school system would hire a teacher that incompetent I'm sure, but the church does it all the time.

Churches are filled with people who are up in front of other people pretending they know something that they don't. Churches hire preachers they don't know, musicians that are just passing through, and almost anybody who can raise their voice real loud and keep a tune at the same time. This isn't the church that Jesus said He would build- this is the drama club. Many church leaders of today know that what I'm saying is true, but they're so deeply involved, and have compromised so much, and with so many people ,until they can't stop playing the game, or pulling the curtain for the next performance. People are hurting really, really bad, but the religious gong show must go on. The reason the show must go on is because most of the performers are hurting inside themselves, and hurting people will continue to hurt people.

Church is a community- not and immunity!

People who fail to perceive the distinction between what the purpose of church is and enter God's glorious Kingdom will always hurt for some reason or another. It's not the church, or Jesus' church, that's causing the hurt, but it's "churchanity." Churchanity is created by those who stay in the first grade all their life. They're frustrated and hurting because they won't apply themselves and move to the next grade or level. You're not immune from hurt because you're in the church. Church is a community, or a common unity, a city where goods and services are provided. A city desires to make progress and help people to live better. Saints are supposed to progress "through" the community of church and into the Kingdom of God. You'll always hurt as long as you stay in church, or keep the "churchy" mentality.

I don't know how much attention you've given to the great number of hurting people that there is today both in the church and in society, but maybe you should. If you're a pastor or a counselor, or if you just love to help people, you probably have spent countless numbers of hours with people who are hurting so deeply until they just can't move on in life. I'll bet some of you have tried everything you know and nothing seems to work. You've given people the Word, you've given them the things to do in order to overcome, and you've prayed with them forever and ever, but they find it so hard to commit to what you say. All across the country men and women of God are hosting workshops, conferences, encounters, and weekly studies aimed at trying to bring healing to hurting people. They don't assume to have all the answers-they simply want to help.

I don't propose to have all the answers either, but I do believe that within the Kingdomgarten atmosphere there is love without boundaries, and acceptance without criticism. A Kingdomgarten environment can only be established by those who are willing to love unconditionally. In this environment you're not trying to fix anyone's problem, but you're so happy that they're there until they actually feel safe to open up and talk themselves through their own issues. A Kingdomgarten environment is a safe environment. No one can manufacture this environment because it can only be facilitated by the willingness of all those who freely choose to surrender to it. The proud and grown up are welcome, but most times they won't come. This book is written in a very simple and understanding language in hopes that Christian and non-Christian people alike will see what I'm talking about and laugh some, cry some, and live better.

The History of Kindergarten

Fredrich Froebel was known as the "Father of Kindergarten" because he developed the first kindergarten in Germany in 1837. Many of the theories and practices developed by Froebel are still being used in Kindergarten classrooms throughout the world today. Froebel stressed that children have playtime to support learning. This is a point that I'll enlarge upon throughout the book. Kindergarten should be a place for kids to grow and learn from their social interaction with other kids.

Froebel of course was German, and the Germans believed that he was out of his mind to believe that children actually learned from having fun, so they wasted no time in burning his book on the philosophy and theory of how children learn.

Froebel was a motherless child. His Mother died before he was one year old. His father raised him and his other two brothers, but he barely had time for them. Young Fredrich had a yearning for something that seemed impossible to quench. He would spend hours upon hours in the beautiful gardens that surrounded his home. Nature became his home and would influence his work and life's accomplishments.

Today we know kindergarten to be a form of pre-school education in which children are taught through creative play, social interaction, and natural expression. I believe that Froebel was correct concerning his views about how children learn, and that these things are true of all children regardless of race or culture. I want to go a step further, however, and say that just because children leave kindergarten, fun and interaction should not stop. If these things are true for kindergarteners then they are also true God's Kingdomgarten kids. Who in the world burned up all of our books about making learning fun in the church?

Whether it's in church or in classrooms, learning was meant to be fun and exciting. I have many fond memories from the twenty six years that I spent in the educational arena, but I remember one year that wasn't so particularly fun. It was when my oldest son was in elementary school. He attended the same school where I taught. His teacher that particular year was nearing retirement, but should have already retired, and every day was a challenge. Elementary children are filled with energy and enthusiasm, and are curious about the world around them, but something as simple as taking them outside to play was a real task for this teacher. She was too mean and tired to supervise their play time, so she kept them inside and yelled at them. Unfortunately, this teacher was tenured.

Tenure can be a brutal two-edged sword. It's actually good for educators who give their best to their profession, but it allows incompetent educators to hide out and pretend they're teaching. It does major damage to poor innocent children. My son survived that year of his elementary year, but it was indeed a struggle.

Regardless of how old we've become, whether we teach in private or public schools, or in church settings- teaching and learning should be fun. We're never too old to learn, and we're never too old to have fun.

With this being said I'd like to propose a definition for kingdomgarten: Kingdomgarten is the childlike attitude and spirit that all of God's kids must have in order to see His mighty kingdom flourish in their lives. The kingdomgarten attitude should remain with us throughout our lifetime. I believe that we make a horrible mistake in church and in society when we assume that just because people reach a certain chronological age that creativity, social interaction, fun and games, and natural expression are no longer needed. God is the author and the giver of every good and perfect gift, so why do so many people think that church, school, and work in general, have to be boring? Simply put, some people who have been thrust into leadership roles should have never been considered. They may have been great serving in support roles but should have never been piloting the plane.

Life is indeed filled with many difficulties, so we must learn to be cheerful as often as we can. Learning to be a kingdomgarten kid is by no means denying the realities of life, but I honestly believe that people live longer and happier when they don't carry stuff over from one day to the next. Being a kingdomgarten kid is not just a book that I've written, but it's actually a lifestyle and a mindset that people should aspire to.

This book is not the impetus for a three-day workshop where the facilitators try to show you how to become kingdomgarten kids. If you're hearing what I'm saying within the pages of this book, then God is already working in you and breaking your pride and arrogance down to the lowest common denominator so that He'll be able to impart anything into you that He so desires. As we become Kingdomgarten kids we'll see more miraculous things happen right before our eyes. Healing for physical body will come to many as they become children (in malice) once again. Broken marriages and shattered dreams will see glorious restoration as pride and ego vanish in His presence. Businesses will flourish once again as people get back to treating other people the way they want to be treated; we'll see a genuine care and concern for who people are and how they feel, rather than just want them to spend money in our store and then tell others about us. Have we become so proud and grown up in this great country of the United States of America that we refuse to humble ourselves and sit at the feet of great men of our time?

Lee Iacocca revived the Chrysler Corporation back in the 1980's because he knew that people were not necessarily motivated by extrinsic rewards like promotions and pay raises. People must be appreciated for who they are and not just for what they can do. Some of life's greatest leaders are not mentioned in the encyclopedias of our day.

In his book, Where Have All the Leaders Gone?, Mr. Iacocca points out that every true leader should possess curiosity, creativity, communication, character, courage, conviction, charisma, competence, and common sense. When you see these qualities in any leader, whether it be a president, a pastor, a congressman, schoolteacher, a secretary, a church minister, or whomever, always applaud them because you won't make it very far without them. One of the most outstanding qualities of a child is his curiosity, so if the new leader has forgotten what it's like to be filled with "childlike" wonder, you might want to reconsider hiring him. We have an old quip that says "curiosity is what killed the cat", but curiosity is not what killed the cat, it's what got him a new home, a loving new owner to love and snuggle under, and delicious meals to eat inside a nice safe environment instead of searching for crumbs in a back alley.

Aren't you curious about what lies beyond church? Aren't you ready to experience once again the joy and pleasure of being a child at heart? Kingdomgarten kids enjoy life far more fully than "churchified" grown-ups.

Chapter One
Lead by Relational Influence

Everything in life will either succeed or fail based on leadership. Someone has to answer the question as to who's in charge? Once you get a social security number the IRS says that you're in charge. The IRS has your social security number so it looks like you're in charge of certain things for sure. If the government owes you money they'll give it to you, but if you owe them they expect you to pay, and if you don't they have ways and means to collect. So, it's fair to say that you're in a leadership position when it comes to paying your taxes. You may not like to pay attention to other people but you're going to pay your taxes. Oh yes, you don't have to have a title like pastor, teacher, professor, doctor, foreman, principal, or superintendent in order to be called "leader".

When you arrived on this planet you were born into a leadership position. Now there is a particular order that God established that everyone can benefit from, providing they submit to it, that causes things to flow a whole lot better. If you'd like to hear it, here it goes: "But I would have you know, that the head of every man is Christ; and the head of the woman is the man; and the head of Christ is God (1 Corinthians 11:3). Boy how I 'd like to tell you how the church has made a big mess out of this one-just keep reading because I probably will. Now this is God's original plan for life, liberty, and the pursuit of happiness, but I already hear some of you saying, "I don't believe in God, so don't talk to me about some man leading me". Well, I can't help if Adam and Eve messed it up; God is not apologizing to anyone for His original plan and purpose for life. Just because you and your buddies don't believe what God said doesn't make it any less true for those who do believe.

Many people don't accept God's order for life because they've witnessed abuse from people, and men in particular, who were supposed to care for and protect them in life. Men are predestined by God to lead. If a man takes a wife he is commanded by God to care of and love his wife. Women are predestined by God to be helpers in the leadership process. If a woman receives a husband she is commanded by God to respect and submit to her husband. The true model of leadership is to lead by relational influence.

Submission must be Mutual

Leadership by relational influence has remained a secret in the church for the most part because it commands mutual submission from all involved. The all time greatest example of leading by relational influence is God the Father, Jesus the Son, and the Holy Spirit. When people hear this statement, they say, "Yeah, I know that, but they were perfect, and we can't live like that today". Many people feel justified when they make statements like this, especially when they look at the way church folk cut up. The very folk who are supposed to show the lost world what God looks like are acting like total heathens. No, even on our best day we are going to mess up. I didn't mean to hurt your feelings but I surely did, and I know that even though I've apologized, you still bear the pain. God knows that we're a mess, but He still expects us to handle our mess among ourselves and not publish it.

The church today is in the news for all the wrong reasons. Divorce, domestic abuse, gays in the pulpit, extortion, tax evasion, adultery, and all manner of evil are constantly being reported happening down at the local church. Even though these things are happening among people who say they love God and one another also, you won't be able to use any of them as your personal excuse for not getting to know God (Romans 1:20). Don't assume that you know God and can't know Him any better. Don't assume that you know your wife, your husband, or your children like you ought to. Jackie and I have been married for thirty-five years and we're still discovering things about each other. Jackie often says that couples study everything else in life but they fail to study one another. People study the bible, the weather, the stock market, they study for exams, and preachers even study for exams, but fail to study each other. How else can a husband dwell with his wife if he does not have knowledge of her (1 Peter 3:7)?

A teacher must study and really get to know her students if she is to get the very best out of them. Those who lead must also make themselves available to the ones they lead so that they may get to know them also. Mutual submission says that whatever service or act you render unto me I am more than willing, regardless of my title or position, to render likewise unto you. Even if I'm not physically or financially able to do the service, in my heart I'm more than willing to. The leader shouldn't have to mop the office floor but he should be willing to.

Obedience alone can become legalistic and kill relationships. People can discern if your heart is not into what you're doing. That's why God says in Isaiah 1:19, "If you be willing and obedient, you shall eat the good of the land". God places willingness before obedience when it comes to our relationship with Him and with one another. Maintaining a Kingdomgarten spirit as you move through life will always have you in position to serve others regardless to whether they'll ever be able to do the smallest thing for you. Kingdomgarten kids operate in the heart of the scripture that says, "And whosoever will be chief among you, let him be your servant (Matthew 20:27)."

Fathers are supposed to Affirm

I believe that a powerful key to leading by relational influence is affirmation. A good natural example of affirmation can be seen at sporting events such as basketball or football when the cheerleaders, and this includes fans also, yell, cheer, and root for their team. Affirmation is a big amen to who you are as a person, and to what you are doing and becoming in life. It assigns value to a person. God affirmed us when He created us by "blessing" us and speaking words over us concerning what we were to do and who we were to become.

God is very relational. He loves His children. He loves us so much until even after we'd sinned and gone astray, He comes to us in human form (Jesus) to live among us and show us how to help affirm others in the same manner He affirmed us. This is the very essence of relational influence. It's a shame that men and women can sit in church and shout amen to what the preacher is saying but refuse to say amen at home to their own children. Home was designed to be the place where parents (relational leaders) affirmed their children. The tragedy today is far too many parents lack affirmation themselves.

If you're thinking that affirmation is accomplished by conversation then you're missing it. Affirmation is accomplished for the most part by demonstration and not by conversation. Children do indeed hear what parents and other authority figures are telling them but at the end of the day they remember what we do, or how we behave. Today, we as a nation are reaping the whirlwinds of societal dysfunctionalism because we've sown to the winds of popular opinion by telling our children to do as we say do and not as we do. By now perhaps you've discovered that children do what they see you do. Don't waste another second sitting around trying to figure out why your children do the numb skull things they do. I know that you probably didn't do any of the wild stuff that your children and other family members do, and it may not even be your fault that they're doing them, but set a good example for them to follow.

There's a spiritual reason involved that sounds something like this: God visits the iniquities of the fathers upon the children unto the third and fourth generation of them that hate me (Exodus 20:5b). This simply means that you, in your particular generation, have an opportunity to answer the call of God and serve Him. If you choose not to do so, God says that He will guarantee you that there will be people in your "generations" (children, grand-children, great grand-children) who will hate Him and will sin worse than you ever imagined sinning. This is why we must affirm by demonstration, and not by conversation alone. A picture is worth more than a thousand words. When Paul was working to affirm the saints at Corinth he reminded them that his speech and his preaching was not with enticing words of man's wisdom, but in demonstration of the Spirit and of power (1 Corinthians 2:4). He wanted their faith to stand, or be firm, in the power of God and not in the wisdom of men.

The word "firm" is the root word of the word affirmation. When something is firm it is solid, strong, or unwavering. People that are firm are not shaky, flaky, or watery. Fathers must affirm their children. Paul was a father to the church at Corinth. This is why after they'd forgotten who they were, and who their father was also, he sent Timothy, his affirmed ministry son, to where they were so that they would have a real live picture of what God's order looked like. Paul knew that they needed "firming up", or else they'd return to their former lusts and sins.

Affirmation is about giving people the real help that they need. It's caring more for someone's being than for their feelings. It's helping children and adults as well, to face up to the realities of life, and also to accept the consequences of their behavior. God is a good Father, and He wants good fathers in the earth so that His will can be done in earth as it has already been done in heaven. Many fathers of the past have fallen asleep and as a result have left many men fatherless and un-affirmed.

Fathers must understand that sin is the total breakdown of who a person is. Sin messes us up spiritually, mentally, physically, socially, sexually, psychologically, and every other way you can think of. All of the degrading sins that men commit today were mentioned in the bible. God mentioned them because in His foreknowledge He knew that men would commit them (Leviticus

18). God knows what's in men so He made sure that it was in His book, the bible. God knew that men would become so defiled that they would have sex with others of the same sex, as well as with animals. He knew that men would become serial killers and mass murderers. He knew that men would get so strung out on drugs that they would sell their own spouses and children for sex just to support their habit. He knew that that the double mindedness in man would manifest itself exposing men who were husbands by day, and "down low brothers" by night. We just recently started referring to it as "down low", but it's been going on for years. Fathers, and I mean the male of the species, must affirm their children or the streets will do it for them. To be totally honest with you, a man doesn't even need children if he's in doubt about his own sexual identity, because only when a man is affirmed himself can he truly affirm his own children.

A child's affirmation is the most important aspect of their life. If you look around at the myriad of problems we're facing today you can see just what I'm talking about. Regardless of all the tendencies and problems that many people say they're born with, the real truth is that every person born into the world was born male or female, boy or girl. God's original plan was for every child to receive affirmation in every area of life, including sexuality. A male may have been born with female tendencies but a quick trip to the bathroom, or stand looking into a mirror, will confirm his maleness.

Fathers are supposed to protect children from sexual predators. A great number of practicing gay and lesbian people today were sexually and emotionally violated as small children and were never able to recover. We should be thankful, however, for the many testimonials of those who have recovered and are doing well, and are also helping others who are struggling trying to recover.

During the ten years of my life that I served as an elementary school principal I witnessed firsthand the struggle that young mothers and grandmothers in particular experienced as they tried to raise their children. It seems that someone has sounded a decree that says, "Raising children is a woman's job". God's plan was, and still is, for a daddy and a mommy to raise a child, and not the entire village. Men must take the lead in this area. I was always thankful for the few men who were supportive of their kids. Men should know that they're not doing anything special when they affirm their children.

Affirmation is a special thing, but please don't look for points because you're doing it- it's what God expects you to do. Men, however, do what they want to do. A good example of this could be seen, and still can today, at the number of people who come to school PTO meetings, science fairs, parents day and other events involving their children. No, not a lot of parents, men especially, show up for the things that they really need to be there for, but I've seen parents take two and three days off work to attend the state high school basketball play offs.

I know it's important to be there when your child is playing sports, but because you're not there for meetings that pertain to his academic pursuit, you're sending the wrong message. You're telling your child that he's no good beyond sports. You're telling her that you're only interested in her because she's good in sports. You're affirming the wrong things. Your child is a person and not a sports star. I'm afraid that many people only want children because they think children are going to make them rich by playing sports. It's a terrible feeling to find out that the very people who are supposed to love you unconditionally only love you for what you can do in the gym, or on the field, and not for whom you are. It's a shame that we're shocked and excited whenever a father shows up for his child's school function or recital. This only goes to show how far from what God intended to be the norm we've drifted. The male is the key to affirmation. The devil knows that the man is the key so he does everything he can to steal the man's identity, kill the man's dreams, or completely destroy him.

Don't Reject God's Pattern: Affirm or Infirm

There are countless numbers of males who are still living at home being taken care of by their mothers. At thirty- five and forty years of age they're still being provided for by their mothers. Mothers will still be there when fathers have failed. If men are not affirmed, or made firm and solid, they're automatically infirmed, or made weak and sickly. Men are weak and sickly today because we refuse to accept God's original plan for the human race. God's plan is non-negotiable- affirm or infirm.

The original man did not come from woman. God put Adam to sleep and took the woman from his side. Adam was the one who said that she shall be called "woman" (Genesis 2:23). She was like the man but yet she was different. Adam was affirmed by God as His delegated authority in the earth. The woman that God gave to him was given to assist him in bringing to pass what God had spoken. Every problem that men and women have ever had or will ever encounter all go back to the day when Adam gave affirmation to the wrong idea. I don't know what was on Adam's mind when he took the forbidden fruit from his wife's hand and ate it, but maybe he knew that she would surely die and rather than being "alone" once again he decided that he would just die with her; Anyway, we've been eating, fighting each other, and dying ever since.

Whether men (the male of the species) know it or not we've been given delegated authority by God to take the lead in having dominion in the earth. His woman (wife or female of the species) is to be by his side to help him in the dominion process. This is God's order or pattern. This is why the bible says that "he" who finds a wife finds a good thing (Proverbs 18:22). Since marriage was given to us by God and is an honorable thing for all people to do, and not just Christians. God actually gives His favor to those who enter this covenant.

Now here's the problem: There is a natural contention between the sexes because of sin. Men who are ignorant of God's ways will try to exert rule over women in a ruthless way, or they will sit back and wait for the woman to do everything. Women, on the other hand who don't know the love of God will quickly say, "Ain't no man gonna rule me, or they'll allow men to dog them out. So what's the answer to this ongoing dilemma? I believe that when God created us, He spoke the word of affirmation over us. We were like Him. We were free moral agents. We were sustained by the life of God. Even after we sinned God became flesh in Jesus and lived among us and delivered the Word of affirmation to us again. Now after He has affirmed us we are to go and affirm others (2 Corinthians 5:17-21). Now, we must remember that anything that God speaks over us must become a process in us.

Affirmation is Regaining One's True Identity

Jesus didn't just come to save us from the torment of hell fire, but He came to save "that" which was lost, and "that" which was lost was our true identity (Luke 19:10). He didn't come to save "he" that was lost, but "that which was lost. Man lost his mind and now he has to be "re-minded". When man lost his mind he also lost his identity. Identity theft is the number one crime of all time. Our true identity was secured in the truth that we were created in His image and His likeness (Genesis 1:26-27). They were already like Him, but they ate the forbidden fruit in hope of being, or becoming, like Him.

Trying to find your true identity in anything other than Christ is an endless pursuit of misery, pain, and utter disappointment Identity theft is a serious crime. People who get caught stealing someone else's identity are prosecuted and put in jail. If you think that identity theft is all about money and credit cards then you're short of your own identity. Oh yes, I know that there are people who are too lazy to work and make an honest living, and are just satisfied with taking money from someone else, and at the same time realize that if they get caught they'll spend time in jail, so it has to be deeper than money. The real problem is that people who steal other people's identity, or possessions, are simply not pleased with who they are. On the surface you're stealing because you think you just need money to buy stuff with, but deep inside you needs and desire to become someone else. People fall asleep at night with the hope of waking up the next day being a totally new person. Money and things come and go, but man's true identity can only be found in Christ

Leading by relational influence requires that you be comfortable in the skin God wrapped you in. Jesus was comfortable with who He was and was never threatened by whom or what others thought He was. He was no less Jesus when He sat by the fireside and chatted with the disciples. The disciples didn't lose respect for Him because He ate with them. Jesus even asked them to do some of the things that He very well could have done Himself. Jesus related to the men He led. He talked about fishing, collecting taxes, building houses, planting crops, and raising sheep. He would often ask them questions and would allow them opportunity to give responses. Jesus was assured of who He was and never hid behind a title. He led by relational influence. God expects for us to be relational and not religious. I don't know why people refer to Christianity as a religion because God never has. Religion is what men profess, or say, that God is.

Chapter Two
Pure Religion vs. Vain Religion

Religion is merely a "profession", because it is completely empty of life. Religion is cold, mean and numb. Paul referred to his former way of living as a Pharisee as a "religious sect" (Acts 26:5). He lived a strict religious life, be he was strictly lost. In the first chapter of Galatians he talks about how he profited in the Jews' religion more than many other of his peers. James 1:26-27 denotes a difference between "vain religion" and "pure religion". The person who just runs their mouth all the time is fooling himself and practices a vain religion, but the person who shows sincere compassion to widows and orphans and keeps themselves unspotted from the world has a pure religion.

Religion refers to a devout practice. Usually when people ask what religion are you they want to know if you're Baptist,

Methodist, Presbyterian, Catholic etc. And that's just what these names are—religious organizations. There is not even one religious organization that can guarantee a relationship with God, not one. There are many religious organizations that preach and teach that Jesus is the way to God, and indeed Jesus is the way to God the Father, but never will anyone find God in the name of the church or organization. If you want to be relational don't ask people what denomination, belief, faith, or religion they are. You'll get a truer answer if you just ask them who they are. I'm convinced that people are tired, hound dog tired of dead vain religion.

Today is March 9, 2009 and I'm reading an article by Rachel Zoll in the Anniston Star (Anniston, Alabama Newspaper) entitled Survey: More Americans say they have on religion. The report came from the Program on Public Values at Trinity College in Hartford, Conn. 54,461 adults were surveyed in English or Spanish from February through November of last year (2008). The survey has a margin of error of plus or minus 0.5 percentage points. The findings were part of a series of studies on American religion by the program that will later look more closely at reasons behind the trends. The article goes on to say that traditional organized religion is playing less a role in many lives. Thirty percent of married couples did not have a religious wedding ceremony and 27 percent of respondents said they did not want a religious funeral. The report just verifies what most people already know, and that is that people are sick of denominations and organizations that hold membership in a religious group which seeks to exercise control over them locally.

Many people are simply fed up with dead religion and are realizing that God's church was never meant to be set in a denominational order in the first place. Well, anyone with normal intelligence can read the New Testament and see that. I think that perhaps denominations started out in innocence and have become something other than what was planned, however I' don't think that leaving your denomination is necessarily the answer. You can find Jesus at the local bar and grill, but in order to enter the kingdom you'll have to come through the womb of the church. The church, however, is out of order. God is a God of order and alignment. The Lord our God is one God, but He is not alone. God the Father, God the Son, and God the Holy Ghost all three dwell together in a perfect harmonious relationship. They're perfectly aligned. There's no confusion about their roles. Where they live everything is settled.

God put the first man, Adam on the earth to exercise His dominion and authority in the earth. He and his wife Eve were to be the means by which the whole earth would be populated with God's offspring. They failed in completing their assignment; they got evicted from the garden, but God covered their nakedness with animal skins. The only reason they're covered (temporarily) is because in eternity the Lamb, or God the Son, has already been slain for the sins of mankind.

God's will must be done in earth as it has already been done in heaven. God is not a man that He should tell a lie (Numbers 23:19). If He has spoken a thing it shall surely come to pass. People who are looking for an excuse to not believe in God are always saying things like, "if God knew that Adam would fail why He put more than one tree in the garden, or why did He create him in the first place?" My answer to questions like these is that God is not like you. He's not afraid to give us choices. He already knows what choice you'll make, and HE truly desires that you'll make the righteous choice, but even if you don't He still sets life and death before you. Jesus wasn't drafted to die for our sin- He volunteered to give His life. God's will be done in the earth.

God meant for the entire earth to be populated with people who would have dominion and power beneath Him. Through the union of a man and a woman who were married to each other God would fill the earth with children-His children. Because of this order, Jesus, or God the Son, must now come through the birth canal of a woman and introduce the kingdom of God, or the rule and reign of God from heaven in the earth. Since all men have sinned and fallen short of God's glory, the Holy Ghost comes down to earth and overshadows a virgin, a woman that has never had sex with a man, named Mary, and she conceives a son and calls Him Jesus, Emanuel, God is now on earth with us again. God has once again come down in the cool of the day to talk with us. Jesus, the Son of God, the express image of the Father, has now come into the earth to complete what was already done in heaven. He comes and introduces the kingdom of God, exposes the kingdom of darkness, and defeats the devil by dying on a cross. In between all of these events He preaches, teaches, heals sick people, and trains and commissions His disciples. Jesus declares that all men who believe in His name shall be saved and inherit eternal life. All the while that Jesus walked on the earth HE constantly and consistently talked about the kingdom of heaven or kingdom of God. He knew that men would have problems in understanding what the kingdom was, so He would often use objects in their own world that they were familiar with to help them understand. When He told them about the kingdom they assumed that HE was a king, and rightly so He was, but He wasn't the kind of king the assumed He was, and neither was His kingdom an earthly kingdom. Things today haven't changed a whole lot. People still don't understand His kingdom. Jesus talked a lot about the kingdom and His Father, but very little about the church. In fact when He opens His mouth He says, "Repent, for the kingdom of heaven is at hand". He doesn't say, "Repent, for the church is at hand", but the kingdom is at hand!

Today, men talk a whole lot about the church, but very little about the kingdom. The most important thing that Jesus did say about the church, and men have forgotten this, is that He would build His own church. The church is His body, and you can't build another man's body for him. He would build His church on the basis of relational influence, the same order of the Godhead. The first Adam failed, but the last Adam won't. God put the first Adam to sleep and took his wife out of his side. Jesus is put to death, another form of sleep, on a wooden cross and blood and water comes flowing from His side to signify the birth of His wife, the church. Jesus' death on the cross is not just a crucifixion-it's a marriage. Every couple that gets married looks forward to their time together to consummate their marriage. He gave His life for you and paid the price for you at the cross. When you gave your life to Jesus, the Holy Ghost broke open the hymen of your unbelief and lodged Himself into your innermost being, and now you carry inside you the seed of God- shucks you are the seed of God. His Word, the original seed lives in you. Even if you decide not to be His wife, He will love you from the pit of hell. God is love. God loves the world (the people whose minds were against Him) so much (or in such a manner) that He gave His only Son, (the one who was in relationship with Him)) that whoever (man, woman, boy, girl) believes (in your heart and saying it with your mouth in Him, the name above all names) Jesus shall be saved (brought out of darkness and into the marvelous light.)

The world has billions of people in it today, but from God's view there are only two people, or two men, on the planet-the first Adam and the Last Adam-Jesus. Now don't run off feeling left out because I have good news for you. You're either hid with God in Christ, or you are alive in Adam's nature. In Adam all men are failures, or all men come short of what God intended. In Christ I have become a new creation and now can have relationship with God. God will teach me how to lead by relational influence. His love has come down (the vertical aspect of the cross) to me so that it may go out (the horizontal aspect of the cross) from me to others. God never asks us to do anything until He has been "with" us

God wants to have a relationship with us, and not just look at us as mere numbers. He wants to be with us in all we do. Parents must desire to be with their children, and not just watch them grow up "doing" stuff. How in the world will your child ever know who you are if he is never allowed to be with you? When I say "with" you I don't just mean in the same house or room with you physically, but with you physically, emotionally, psychologically, mentally, in mind, body, and spirit. When you're "with" someone your mind isn't on all the other stuff you've got to do. You don't take a book and read it at your child's ball game or music recital. You don't read the paper while having dinner with your wife. You don't clip your nails while watching a movie with your spouse. You don't yawn and look uninterested when your child is talking to you about something that's really an issue for them. The CEO should never throw his weight around when workers want to talk about work related issues. The relational leader, whether it's a parent, a boss, a teacher, a pastor, or any leader in any capacity, will seldom have to use the phrase, "because I said so!" Most of the times when we hear people say that we're to do something because they said so, it suggests that they're frustrated, tired, in a hurry, can't really explain why, don't know why, insecure in their identity, or just plain mean. It takes time for relationships to develop, and most people don't think that they have enough time, but for those who place a high premium on developing good relationships, God will surely redeem the time.

Chapter Three
Idle, Idol Titles

Leaders who refuse to go on to know the Lord will never truly know who they are and could remain hidden behind their titles forever. Titles are idle. They don't move, breathe, and live. People don't form or build relationships with titles. Titles can also become idols. An idol is anything that gets between us and the God who created us and steals the fondest affection of our heart from Him. It could be a person, a job, a pleasure, an automobile, an animal, a lust of the flesh, and even your title or position. People aren't interested in the titles and position we hold as leaders; they want to know who we are. The problem is that people who think more of themselves than they ought to because of their title or their spiritual gifts, aren't very relational at all. Their leadership style is just telling people what to do, or, if not that they will micro-manage everything.

Leaders who have received their kingdomgarten education and have gone on to complete the other requirements of continuous education, but yet have retained the kingdomgarten spirit, understand how important it is to establish relationships with the people they work with and lead. Relational leaders take their work serious, but they take themselves not so serious. The work is God's work, but you're just you. We've been commanded by God to love everybody regardless of who they are or what they call themselves. We don't have to eat, sleep and drink with everybody, but we must surely love them. Sometimes people are fine with you until they find out that you're not the same color as they are, that your church denomination is different, they're of a different political party, they're for Alabama and you're for Auburn, or that you belong to a different fraternity or sorority than they. It's a shame that people have to gather all this information about you in order to decide if they like you or not. It's truly sickening.

Many church leaders are so sick with themselves today until they can't even sit at the table with people who don't have titles, and it had better be the correct title at that. Perhaps there has never before a period in history when people have been so title conscience than our present time. People are so hungry for a title until if you don't give them a title, they'll dub themselves with one. There's no title that you could possibly give yourself that will make up for all you lack in character and integrity. The saints at Corinth certainly didn't lack spiritual gifting, but they fell way short in character and integrity. Just like the idolatrous background they came out of where they bowed down and worshipped almost anything you could name, they were now doing the exact same thing in the church with their titles, gifts, and callings. They were being carried away with dumb idols even as they were led (1 Corinthians 12: 2). So many ministry people today like the Corinthians of old are sick with wanting to be recognized. They believe that a title will take them places and gain them fortune and fame. Pastors of small churches with twenty to fifty people believe that if they can just get a "big name" preacher or singer to come to minister at their church, then that's all they need for their breakthrough. After all, if they (the big timers) can preach and sing on TV so can we. This lust for recognition puts a tremendous strain on the people who support leaders who think like this because they'll have to be the ones who divvy up the money to bring in the big-time preacher boys and girls. I'm not saying that we shouldn't have guest ministry to come in and bless the people, but you ought to bring in those that you're in relationship with and that you can afford to bring in. You have thirty-five people in your congregation and they all work at Wal-Mart, the local chicken plant, and the furniture factory; it's just not sane to bring in people you know you can't afford to bring in. Besides that, you don't know what all you'll have to clean up after they've come and preached things you had no idea they'd preach. In spite of all the warnings that God sends us we still insist on being "big".

The small-time preacher can't wait to get big so that he can have two armor bearers following him around everywhere. But hold on, you don't have to pastor thousands in order to have armor bearers; you can call yourself a Bishop and have your armor bearers right now. Hey, what's his name across town did it. Now please understand that there's absolutely nothing wrong with men having titles, it's what happens to the wrong people who get titles and don't possess character and integrity that sickens everything. You see, once you get your beloved title and promotion to pastor, bishop or apostle, all of a sudden you can no longer play ball with the saints anymore, or just sit around and chat with them. On the other hand now if you were a kingdomgarten saint, pastor, bishop, apostle, or presiding prelate, you could have all the fun you wanted to have with the saints and not be thought less or more of one bit. That's because you knew who you were and so did the saints.

We're all saints regardless of our titles. It's not much fun having a kindergarten teacher who sits at the desk all day long and refuses to get on the floor and help the kids put the puzzle back together. By the same token it's no fun having church leaders who have become their titles and sit around looking like permanent monuments-shucks; many have already become pillars in the temple of God. In their own minds they've become idols. They expect other people whom they believe to be peons to bow down and give obeisance to them and the illustrious titles they bear. I've witnessed many classroom teachers who thought way too much of their degree and the title they bore. In fact, this was probably the reason they were so boring. They strutted around with the attitude that said, "I've got mine and you have to get yours." People like this have really forgotten everything they learned in kindergarten.

Titles Don't Reach Hearts

You have to reach children before you can teach them, and a title has never reached anyone before. Why would a teacher or leader want to make life miserable for others anyway? The money certainly isn't that great, so what's the motivation? Could it be that somebody made life miserable for you as you were growing up and now you want to exact revenge? Stop teaching today and get a life! If you think that the public-school classrooms across

America are messed up then you should take a look at what goes on in most churches.

Most saints with gifting take themselves far too serious. Please don't get me wrong, the work of God should never be taken lightly, but please remember that the greatest work God is doing is the work that He's doing inside of us as He conforms us to the image of His dear Son. The main idea in teaching and leading is to reach the hearts of those you teach or lead. It takes courage to reach hearts. Titles may affect the minds of people but they'll never affect their hearts. One of my favorite lines in the movie "Braveheart" is the line where Mel Gibson says: "Men don't follow titles, but they follow courage." Titles don't seek to form relationships with people, but people who understand who they are, will.

Church is the special relationship that believers have with Jesus and with one another. It was intended to be a safe relationship. One in which we could agree, disagree, laugh, cry, and love each other unconditionally. Mutual submission is the absolute trademark of our relationships; Husbands to wives, brothers to sisters, employers to employees, teachers to students, and vice versa for all of these. We're to bear one another's burdens and thus fulfill the law of Christ (Galatians 6:2). People who take themselves too serious are not able to help others bear their burdens. They can't laugh or cry. Having fun is out of the question. No, it's not much fun when a loved one or friend dies, but we ought to have certain memories from their lives that bring us to joy and tears. After all, joy and sorrow are part of our hope and experience.

My wife lost her mother, her father, her oldest uncle, a great aunt, a first cousin, and her only sister, all within a fifteen-month period of time, and I watched her express her grief in tears as well as laughter. She would go into the room where her father stayed and just breakdown in tears, but then she would show me how her father would knock on the kitchen door and say, "Jack, it's me, your runaway child coming home", and she would explode with laughter as she demonstrated his mannerisms. My wife has always treasured the scripture that says a merry heart doeth good like a medicine, but a broken spirit drieth the bones (Proverbs 17:22). Jackie, my wife, is the most relational person I know. The people in her life who have her as a friend are more than blessed. She epitomizes the kingdomgarten kid more than anyone I know. She loves and cares deeply, but she laughs and has fun just as deep. When she's hurt or let down she never withdraws her love or sits around and mope. Her love goes right into the hearts of people, not her title as the pastor's wife, or pastor-first lady Jackie.

It's not normal for children to sit in a corner all day with their lips poked out and a sour look on their face. However, this is exactly how many people in the church behave today. When they were small children they were abused by people who were abused by people who were abused by people who...and the list goes on and on all the way back to Adam and Eve, but it doesn't have to continue, because the joy of the Lord has come. The Lord's joy doesn't always mean joy and laughter, but it does mean that even when we're crying, we can be confident that He'll turn our mourning into dancing. So don't sit around with a broken spirit that will surely dry your bones up as dry as the Sahara desert. The bones represent the foundation of your life, and if your foundation is destroyed where will you stand? I have nothing against Toronto, but you really don't have to go there in order to laugh. If you want to laugh right now, get a mirror and look into it! Come on, lay your title down, in fact go flush it down the stool, and then roll on the floor like a five year old ecstatic with laughter.

The beauty of the Kingdom is that the Father has provided everything that pertains to life and godliness for us through the knowledge of His Son. The sad news is that you'll never see it as long as you stay proud and grown up. Kingdomgarten kids will see it because they have shouted, rejoiced, and danced their way out of religion and refuse to be entangled again. Kingdomgarten kids don't fight over positions and titles. To be called "son" is title enough. Since every seed reproduces after its own kind, maybe the church needs a Kingdomgarten five-fold ministry that produces a kingdomgarten ministry of the saints. The ministry of the saints is the missing ministry. It's the army of God that the world has never seen. It's the manifestation of Christ, the head, in His body the Church. It's the saints in their workplaces being confident in whom they are, and not wondering and worrying about whether or not they'll become a big time preacher and finally break into "the ministry" one day. It's the cashier at WalMart, the waiter at McDonald's, the teller at the bank, the policeman, the doctor, the nurse, the factory worker, the lawyer, the PGA golfer, the coach, the athlete, the actor, the singer, it's every saint in every possible working environment doing the jobs they were trained for with the understanding that they are right where God wants them to be and are not trying to "go into the ministry". The only title that the saints need is to fully comprehend that they are "entitled" to the ministry of reconciliation, and that God has planted them into all the world as ministers of reconciliation to reconcile others to Him (2 Corinthians 5:17-21). We are literally "expressions" of God's unconditional love. Titles Outside of the Bonds of Unconditional Love Simply Kill

I offer these as tips for married couples.

1. The titles "husband and wife" won't make your marriage work or save it from disaster.

2. You must learn the essence of "being" a husband and "being" a wife if you are to have success.

3. Respect titles, but crave relationship.

4. Drive pride so far from your home that it couldn't find its way back with a GPS.

5. Break the rules and have fun together. What's more important your budget or your relationship?

6. Since it's the "little foxes" that spoil the vines, learn to think about and do the "little things" that keep producing the rich wine of a healthy marriage.

7. Read together, pray together, work together, walk together, talk together, be silent together, dance together, cry together, laugh together, act silly together, celebrate together.

8. If you've become pre-occupied with each other's faults and shortcomings, find a married couple wiser and more mature than you and make yourselves accountable to them for teaching you the basic principles of Christianity, advanced Christianity, or any subject that focuses on God. Most of the time when Christian couples are experiencing conflict it's because they've lost their focus on Christ.

If God doesn't build the marriage whatever you erect through your own self effort will be shaken to pieces.

Chapter Four
It's Play Time:
"Hey Bishop, Throw Me the Ball!"

During my early school years when we went outside to play it was called recess. Without a doubt it was my favorite time of the day, other than lunch time that is (smile). Recess never lasted quite long enough. By the time we worked up a good sweat it was time to go in. We would always remember the score in our ball game because that's where we would pick up on tomorrow. I shudder to think what school would have been like without a playground.

Today what we called recess is called PE, which is short for physical education. Schools today have gymnasiums where PE is taught as a separate class. Kids even have lockers for changing clothes, as well as a teacher who just specializes in teaching PE. Shucks I never saw a PE teacher until I reached seventh grade. Our classes during my elementary years were self-contained, so our entire day was spent with one teacher. The teacher was with us all the time. She greeted us every morning with a warm smile, she taught us our subjects, and even played with us on occasions at recess. She didn't wear a name tag that said "teacher", be we all knew she was our teacher. It was always a special treat whenever our teacher participated in our play. It didn't matter if the teacher could play as good as we could or not, we always thought it was a big deal.

During my many years as a teacher and a principal I enjoyed mixing it up with my students. I remember that my students would work extra hard in the classroom just to get a little extra time at PE. There are, however many children who hate PE and are totally turned off by the idea of running or doing exercises. It's double jeopardy for students like this when they have a teacher who is the proverbial statue of liberty at PE time. Maybe we should go back to calling it recess because that would give it a different flavor. Recess means to withdraw from, or retreat from. It means to take a break from the ritual of work and chill out. It doesn't necessarily have to mean playing sports or doing physical exercise, even though these are real important. My point is that a teacher is a vital part of a student's life, and can impact the student's life in so many ways.

Children learn better when they work and play together. Teachers must never resign to just being figureheads, but must involve themselves in every way possible to help children learn. They all don't learn by the same method. Meanwhile, down at the local church a similar picture persists. The saints show up to praise the Lord and the big boys sit on the platform and watch. I never thought that much of teachers who just sat at their desk and daydreamed while the children worked, or played. But this is exactly what you see in most churches, unless of course you have leaders who don't hide behind their positions and titles. The saints are down there screaming and peeling paint off the wall and the Bishops are up there trying to get a sermon note. Sadly there are many who see nothing wrong with this arrangement, but I'm speaking out; it needs to breathe its last breath now! We're a kingdom of priests. We all are to minister unto the Lord together. Who incorporated this papal system of worship into God's house? We have but one high priest and His name is Jesus. So come on bishop and teach me how to praise God! No come on, you taught me to be faithful in church, you taught me to tithe and give, so now teach me to praise Him. On no-no, I don't mean tell me how to do it, but I want you to show me how. I want you to take the lead in this thing! I'm throwing you the ball Bishop, and I want you to throw it back to me. You know it's not much fun out on the playground when you throw the ball to someone and they just hold it and stare at it.

And by the way Bishop, why on earth did you show up at the annual church picnic wearing a three-piece suit and tie? What's that all about? You really didn't intend to play ball with us did you? That's why you showed up twenty minutes before the picnic was over isn't it? You're good enough to teach and preach to me but you're too good to play with me, huh? Oh yes, and why did the first lady show up with you to the picnic wearing that after five dress and that wide hat? I know she had to be burning up as hot as it was.

Yeah, I want to talk about this "first lady" thing anyway. Where did this come from? I thought Eve was the first lady. She is your wife isn't she? Well, why don't you just call her honey, sweetheart, or Jenny? And another thing, why does she always have to call you Bishop, even when you're at home? What is your real name anyway? Let me calm down here, I guess it's okay to have all this stuff, but on the other hand it has created a gigantic lust for honor and recognition among people who don't deserve it, and it puts blind and unsuspecting followers under extreme bondage. The religious world is ripe with little boys and jacklegs that are rabid to finally be "over somebody." They've been watching the religious TV channels and have been entertaining visions of grandeur about themselves.

Bishop! I thought I told you to throw me the ball! You see, while you're standing there holding the ball, and trying to look all pretty and stuff, Some young, unsuspecting member of our congregation is forming the wrong perception of who church leaders are and what they do.

Your Family Wants Daddy, not Bishop!

Throw me the ball right now Bishop! And another thing, when you get home tonight, leave your Bishopric in the car, get out and go into your home and be a loving husband to your sweetheart wife. Allow your kids to call you daddy, and not Bishop. I mean no offense to anyone who is a true Bishop, but in my state there is such a lust to be a Bishop that it's maddening. But they won't be Bishop for long because being an Apostle is looking better all the time. Honestly, we have freaked out. Bishop, if you'd just throw that ball there wouldn't be so many men and women in the church divorcing one another. Leaders divorce one another on Saturday, get a nice message together on Saturday night, and preach like nothing happened on Sunday morning. The sad news is that people still show up to see this unfolding drama. Throw the ball Bishop, or that young man who was sexually abused as a child, but has never told anyone, will turn to a homosexual lifestyle. He sees you Bishop, and he knows you're not real. Throw the ball bishop, and maybe you will avoid an extramarital affair.

The Bishop is also a Brother to the Saints

We know you're our leader, our teacher, our overseer, our set man, but please just throw the ball. We won't love you any less if you throw us the ball. We know that you preach all over the world, and you're highly anointed, millions come to hear you, and you have every degree there is to be had, but if you don't throw that ball we may never truly know who you really are-so throw it now! Well, I see that you're going to be stubborn Bishop, so I'm going to have to use the Word on you. Jesus hung out with His disciples, so why won't you hang out with us? He sat and ate with His disciples but you never sit at the table with us. Is it because we don't have titles like big time preachers? I'm trying to entreat you as a brother now Bishop, but you bout to get on my last nerve now! Anyway, the bible says that we are to submit ourselves to one another in the fear of God (Ephesians 5:21). Does that sound like mutual submission to you Bishop? Well, we're submitted to you, but if you don't throw the ball to us, so we question whether you're submitted to us. I bet Jesus and Paul would have thrown the ball. You're not a kindomgarten kid are you Bishop? I'll bet you have forgotten your a-b-c's haven't you? Can you count to ten? Let me hear you do it. Do you say you're sorry when you hurt someone's feelings? Or do you use your title and position to make the ones you offend feel like they're the guilty ones? After all is said and done, we're simply brothers and sisters in the Lord. We're God's kingdomgarten kids.

Chapter Five
The Truth of the Matter

I could go on and on with this scenario but I'll lighten up here. Hopefully you see what I'm driving at. Ministry people are so busy doing what they say God has given them to do until they don't have time to "throw the ball," or build relationships with family or with the people they're supposedly leading. The Bishop can't throw the ball because he's got to "win the lost at any cost," This win the lost at any cost doctrine (and it definitely has become one) has so pervaded the religious world until people don't have time to even hear God. It's a shame but God's people have been held hostage by what theologians "think" about the coming of Jesus. "We don't have but a little time left so we've got to get as many souls saved as possible;" "Any day now He could crack the eastern sky"; "Are your bags packed and ready to go?" These statements, and many more like them, must be understood in context of what the bible says about the appearing of Jesus, and not by just what theologians and commentaries say. The bible is its own commentary. The problem is that most men have lazy minds and this book is surely not one for lazy minds.

Men have used the soon coming of Jesus as an excuse to not build relationships, especially relationships in the body of Christ. What if you gained the whole world and you lost your soul? What if we got so consumed with working for God that we never even got to know Him? Jesus talked about men who did all kinds of exploits "for" God but God never "knew" them (Matthew 7:21-23). These men were not heathen unbelievers, they were men who did their own thing, and never took time to see what the Father really wanted. Woe unto preachers who have won millions to Christ but have offended their own children by not having time to affirm them in who they were and were to become.

Rapture: "We're outta here!"

We've been so busy getting ready for the "Rapture" until we've neglected the body of Christ. The term rapture never appears in scripture, but in the New Testament the Greek term "harpazo" is used. This term implies stealing, dragging off, carrying away, leading away, catching up, catching away, or transporting. It's totally a waste of time and energy to be preoccupied with the rapture that most religious folk talk about all the time. I'm talking about the one where Jesus sneaks in by night and steals all believers away to heaven. The problem with this teaching is that it takes people's minds away from seeing Jesus in the here and now, in His body the church. Christians are walking around just thinking about heaven, and God is thinking about the earth. There's a big problem here, because we're trying to get up and out of here to heaven but God's trying to get down and in the earth. God's work in heaven is all complete, but the earth is still groaning and travailing awaiting the manifestation of the sons of God (Romans 8:19-22).

God has already seated the believers in heavenly places in Christ Jesus (Ephesians 2:6). We're seated in heavenly places in the Lord so that we may see what the will of the Father is and then pray His will be done in the earth as it is already done in heaven. We don't pray from the down-up position, but we pray from the up- down position. We are in constant need of being raptured, or getting caught up. Enoch got caught up, Moses was taken away, Elijah was transported, Jesus prayed in the Garden of Gethsemane (John 17:11) and made the statement to His Father that He was no longer in the world, and He was right there in the garden, Paul was caught up to the third heaven but his body never left earth, and Phillip was divinely transported from the desert to Azotus. My point in giving all these accounts of men getting "caught up" is to suggest to Christians that perhaps we need to get caught up out of the religious mindset that snares us. We need to stop looking for Jesus in the cumulus clouds and begin looking for Him amid the great "cloud of witnesses "that the bible talks about, as well as those who live right in our midst.

Jesus certainly wants to make His appearance, but He wants to make it in His body the church-the people, and not the building. A good friend of mine by the name of Randall Worley has often said that "God is going to rupture your rapture". It needs rupturing because most Christians are so busy trying to get up to heaven and experience glory until they can't really experience the glory that He expects us to release every time we come together. We've been anointed to glorify Him. He gives us power so that we can give Him glory. The world has never seen the saints in glory. The world has seen the saints in confusion, in the news for the wrong things, in disputes over doctrines, and has seen all of the stupid bumper stickers on the back of our cars (Rapture Ready, Honk if you Love Jesus, and In case of the Rapture this car will be unmanned, etc.). There certainly will be rapture, but not before there has been a capture.

The Schizophrenic Body

We don't need to be raptured but we need to be captured. We need God to get our attention so that we can see Him in His body, the church. The greatest sin committed by Christians is failure to discern the Lord's body (1Corinthians 11). I most certainly believe that Jesus is coming for His body, but I also believe that before He comes "for" it, He wants to come "in" it. Foxes have holes, the birds of the air have nests, but the son of man has no place to lay His head. He wants to lay His head on His body, the church, but the church is in a state of schizophrenia. On one hand we're saying have your way Lord, and on the other hand we're saying come on and get us Jesus-we're ready to go home. The reason we're so schizophrenic is because we're still listening to our old head. Let this mind be in you, which was also in Christ Jesus (Philippians 2:5). You can't have his mind unless you've allowed Him to take yours out of the picture. As long as you continue to do your own thing and never repent to the Kingdom of heaven, you'll never have His mind. When we don't have His mind we'll keep working "for" Him as opposed to working "with" Him.

He wants to work in us His will to do. The double minded man is the man who is having delusions, hallucinations, and thought disorders. I believe that "double mindedness" is what Jesus was referring to when He talked about tow people being in one bed, and one of them being taken and the other one being left behind. God will always take the spiritual mind but the carnal mind gets rejected every time. We haven't become kingdomgarten kids because we refuse to allow the Word of God to completely shape our thinking. Consequently we're seeing, hearing, and saying things that God has not declared. God hasn't told you to look for Him in the cumulous clouds before you look for Him in His body that you meet with each week. If all of our visions, dreams, knowledge, and revelation doesn't cause us to become more humble and broken, then we can safely say that God wasn't in it!

One More Thing Bishop!

Now let's get back to the Bishop, because I don't want to leave him hanging. I think that people aspire to be Bishops because they think that Bishops have three, four, or several churches under them. The more churches the more money. I mean no disrespect to Bishops who are genuine in their walk toward God, but I've purposely chosen the "Bishop" because there are those among us who are just greedy for money and control, and don't even understand that the term" Bishop" is not "who" a person is, but rather what he "does"-he oversees from above. I struggle to write these things because I know that the office is real, but on the other hand I know that wherever you have the real you'll have to deal with the pseudo as well.

The Bishop with the revelation of the body of the Lord is the relational Bishop. This Bishop will throw the ball to the saints because he knows that he's a saint also. This man of God wants to see God's people connect to one another. He understands that there is a deposit of God in every saint in the body. The ministry that God gave to the body is commonly referred to as the five-fold ministry. I like to call it the "fist" ministry, because if you ball your five fingers up it forms a fist. The apostle, prophet, evangelist, pastor, teacher ministry must never be isolated; they all must touch each other. The thumb represents the apostle, and obviously the thumb is able to move across your hand and touch the other four very easily. The message here is very simple- there is no true God ordained ministry without the divine commission of the office of the Apostle. While you may be having a shouting good time and doing all kind of wonderful stuff, you'll never have God's government because that's what the commissioned Apostle brings. While the original Apostles are all passed into glory, God commissions men today and sets them into the office to "function" as Apostles. The purpose of the Apostolic ministry is to equip the saints for the work of "their "ministry (Ephesians 4:11-13). The ministry of Ephesians chapter 4 ministers "to" the saints and builds them up, and the saints in turn go and ministers to the world. My whole point is that not one saint is to be left out. Every saint has a supply of the Spirit for the local body of which he is connected to. The Apostle Paul was sent by God, and not by the church at Jerusalem. This great man of God loved all the saints and desired that every saint function in the body of Christ. Paul even referred to Bishops and deacons as saints, and to himself as the least of all saints (Ephesians 3:8).

So many people in ministry today think of themselves more than they ought to. They're simply no concerned about the spiritual growth and development of the people they lead. Like the Bishop who refuses to throw the ball to the saints, many leaders, and including those in corporate America, only want to use people for their own gain. There's so much of this sickness in the church until it makes you just want to throw up. It's called greed and manipulation, and the United States of America is as

I speak is reaping the results of years and years of it. Our only hope is to become kingdomgarten kids. Now here's the question, and also the answer, that I know many people will surely have as a result of what I've said:

Not so Common

Question: What if the Bishop, or any leader for that matter, becomes "common" in the eyes of the people?

Answer: The term "common" in the scriptures refers to something unclean. People with leprosy were called unclean. Animals that were not to be eaten by humans were called unclean. A woman during her menstrual cycle was considered unclean. Jesus, the great Bishop of our soul allowed a woman who was bleeding to touch Him. If the bishop won't throw the ball because he considers himself to be "all of that", and the people to be common, then perhaps he should be seen as common in their eyes. If the people take the leader for granted then shame on them, but if the leader takes the people for granted then shame on him.

Familiarity does often breed contempt, but it doesn't necessarily have to. Do you take your spouse for granted after having been married for so long a time? Whose fault is it if it has happened? Rather than take responsibility for problems that occur in marriage people get divorced. If you have a leader who is worried about becoming common in the eyes of the people then you probably have a person who should not be leading. Moses walked with God's people, he walked in front of them, and he even had to go up above them to hear God. There will always be a Korah in the camp who will try to bring the bishop "down to his size" just to make themselves look bigger. Leaders must know the people that labor among them. Joshua was chosen from among the people. Moses knew Joshua, Joshua knew Moses, and they both knew the people. Please check and double check to assure that the fear of being called common is not really the fear of being transparent and relational.

Chapter Six
Teaching Is a Calling

All of us can learn things from each other. When we gain wisdom and understanding from others it means that they've taught us something, or we've learned something from them. They don't have to bear the title of "teacher." My dad never took out a book and used a blackboard to show me how to work on cars, but I watched him as he did so. He only had a third grade education so all of his knowledge about automobiles had to have come from watching his father and others as they worked on cars and trucks. Working on cars in an informal atmosphere with your child watching you is easy, but standing in a classroom with twenty to thirty bodies looking attentively is all together different.

Knowing the content of subject matter is fairly simple for most of those who teach, but dealing with all the intangibles of the student and teacher relationship is where many jump ship. Regardless of whether you teach day care, pre-school, elementary, junior high, high school, college, graduate, public school, private school, church school, or home school, you should know by now that there's something divine about teaching. At the end of the workday the mechanic leaves the car in the garage, the appliance repair technician leaves the appliance at the shop, and when school is dismissed the children go to their homes, but the teacher takes her struggles home with her; that is, teachers who are called to their profession. I worked as an educator long enough to see teachers who were definitely called as well as teachers who did not love children or people at all. Many people in the church refer to themselves as being called to preach, called to evangelize, or called to pastor, but what most people don't understand is that even lost people were called-everyone is called, everyone is born into this world with certain gifting and interests. God knows what things He placed inside all of us. Formal training helps to prepare us with the academia, but only God can call us.

Ephesians chapter 4:1 states that we are to "walk worthy of the vocation wherewith ye were called." Your vocation is your calling. It's what God has put in you to be and to do in life. God predestined you to "be" who you are in Him. No one else on the entire planet can "be" who you are in Him. Your first calling is to simply be. Whatever you do in life will be a result of who you are and who you were called to be. You don't decide to teach school because you were told by your parents who were also teacher that you need to go into teaching. When you were a child you were supposed to be trained up in the way "you" were to go, and not in the way "your parents wanted" you to go (Proverbs 22:7).

Sometimes parents do dumb things like insisting their children practice the same professions they practice. Years ago at a Career Day program for my fifth graders I had various people from the community come and speak about their professions. One particular speaker from a local college was questioning the kids about what they wanted to do when they grew up, and in his sheer excitement one young boy exclaimed, "I want to be a truck driver!" In his total ignorance of the plans and purposes of God for the lives of all people, the college professor replied, "oh you don't want to be a truck driver!" It's not left up to us to decide what children grow up to become. We can help in the process of their growing up, but what people are interested in becoming is between them and God. By the way, this country would be deadlocked without truck drivers. It's really sad that many religious folk don't view truck driving, building houses, policeman, professional athlete, businessman, or any "secular" occupation as divine callings in life.

Many are called but few are Chosen

"So the last shall be first, and the first last: for many be called, but few chosen" (Matt.20:16). The first calling is to "be", as I have already stated. Your first occupation is to "be" in Him. It is to be called in Him. You need to know that you're in Him before you start trying to figure out what you're going to do. God calls everyone on the planet to a particular occupation and vocation, but the choosing is all dependent upon how we respond to the call. God both calls and chooses. It does not matter what anyone thinks about who God calls and chooses. God knows what He has placed inside of every person born into this world and He will never change His mind about the gifts and callings He has given to us. God already knows before our parents ever decide to get together whether or not we'll respond to His predetermined call on our life.

The gifts and callings of God are without repentance (Romans 11:29). This means that they are irrevocable and that God will never repent or regret that He called you and chose you to do what He has planned for you. God called you and chose you to a certain work in His Kingdom, so don't waste time worrying about what someone else is doing or how much they're making. God wanted you just like He wanted Mary. God called Mary to bring forth Jesus, and Mary was "chosen" form among women, but never forget what Mary said after her call: "Be it unto me according to thy Word" (Luke 1:38). There were other virgins available to God but He chose Mary to give birth to the flesh of God, but not to die for our sins (this is as good a reason not to worship Mary as I could ever think of).

Many people, after they have tried to do other professions and fail, suddenly decide they want to teach. It wouldn't be so bad if they wanted to teach dogs how to sit and fetch- but no, they want to teach human beings, and children at that! I once told a teacher who worked under me that she needed to find the occupation that gave her joy and fulfillment because it was obvious that teaching wasn't it. I told her that she didn't love children and that they knew it. Many children would act up in her class just to get sent out. This teacher was well versed in the content of academia, but was very lacking in the content of her character. Regardless of what or who they teach, the most effective teachers are those whom God has dealt with and broken.

God called and chose Jonah to go to the city of Nineveh and preach, but Jonah had other ideas, so God had to break him down and humble him until he finally delivers God's message. Those who teach must be humble, patient, and full of compassion. How you say what you say is more important than what you say. Perhaps Jonah didn't like the people of Nineveh and probably surmising that they would listen to the message of God and repent, he decided to do something else in life. If you think that God was surprised by Jonah's stubbornness to obey Him then you don't understand who God is. God cannot be shocked or surprised. God has foreknowledge, and He calls all men to be found "in Him", but He already knows which men will accept Him and which men will reject Him. What Jonah didn't do Jesus did do. Jonah spent three days and three nights in the belly of a great fish and still has problems with obedience, but Jesus, the "lamb slain before the foundation of the world" (Rev.13:8), steps out of eternity into time and dots every I and crosses every T, and finishes the work of God. The work that God is doing is in us, and not in the things around us, or in the things we do. We try to find contentment and peace in the things around us, the things we make with our own hands such as the booth that Jonah made (Jonah 4:5), or the gourd that God prepared (Jonah 4:6), but true contentment and peace can only be found in Him. Jonah became so messed up in his mind that he wanted God to take his life from him (Jonah $:3), but that would have been useless, because Jesus had already given His life in eternity past and would come in the fullness of time and give it on a wooden cross. It's funny that Jonah tries to find relief by sitting under a tree while Jesus gives us eternal peace by dying on a tree. We are living in a time when people care more about things than they do people. God knows what's inside of all men. He calls all men, but He chooses men based upon what's inside their hearts. The same God that provides shelter for our heads will send worms to eat the shelter away.

It is only when we have a "childlike" spirit that we become flexible enough for God to use us in situations that we had no desire to be in at all. Sometimes we're so quick to say what we will or won't do, but none of us knows the things that are in us like we ought to, but the more we get to know "Him" the more we become conformed to His image and we find ourselves being used in ways we knew not of.

Become all things to all Men

If a child does not learn the way you teach then you must teach the way the child learns. Just because you teach something there is no guarantee that learning takes place. The teacher who does not learn from their own teaching is not learning to teach. If your teaching is not filled with compassion then you're nothing but an empty wind bag. The teacher who is small in her own eyes is a giant in the eyes of her students. If children can't warm up to you it may mean that you've frozen them stiff. If you're going to teach reading be sure that you're an easy picture to read. If you're going to teach math make sure that you're a whole number and not a "fraction". If you're going to teach science then be sure that you're an open discovery. If you teach chemistry be sure to allow children to experiment in the lab of your heart. If you teach the saints at church be sure that they know that you're the least of all saints, and if you're not a kingdomgarten saint then don't even bother to do it.

You can only become all thing to all people when you realize who you are in "Him". Simply trying to make everyone happy will drive you nuts, but "being" who you're supposed to be to the people that God "sets" in your life's path will reward both you and them. If you have the wrong people in your life, and many people surely do, you'll find yourself constantly frustrated. If you have people in your life who are supposed to be there, and many people do, then stop nagging and picking at them all the time. Only when you "become" who God wants you to "become" can you become all things to the people around you. No matter how hard you try you cannot make this rule work in your flesh.

A Real humorous memory

It's really important not to have too many rules for small children. One rule that you must have as a teacher is that there can be no hitting, touching, or biting allowed. I remember a kindergartner who was sent to my office for persistent biting. I was very much aware of how small children take things literally, but on this particular situation my mind was not in gear. I arose from my desk and positioned myself right in front of this tiny tot and looked her eye ball to eye ball and said, "Now you must never bite anyone again, do you understand me; now read my lips!" What this little girl said in reply are words I shall never forget. She raised her head, while wiping her tears, and said, "I don't see no words on your lips." I said excuse me, and ran into my bathroom and rolled in laughter. I was finished for the day. Art Linkletter was right when he said, "kids say the darndest things!" By the way, I never saw this particular child in my office again for anything.

Parents and teachers both know how important it is to break small children of offensive habits such as hitting and biting. Fortunately, most children do learn to keep their hands, feet, and teeth to themselves, but far too many never do and become menaces to society. Christians bite and devour one another all the time and never say that they're sorry. It's amazing that adults will have small children to apologize for their wrongs but themselves will commit terrible trespasses and act as if nothing ever happened. Yes, I've seen tiny little biters in kindergarten actually draw blood with their bites, but the little blood they drew in no way compares to the serious biting that God's people do to one another.

I want us to take a serious look at how and why Christians treat each other so mean and evil. As I reflect on how I had to deal with notorious little bitters at school I can't help but wish that it was as easy to deal with adult church biters as it was with tiny little kindergarten biters. Christians destroy on another and then they wonder what happened? The bible warns us about biting on each other (Galatians 5:15) but continue to gnaw away at each other like beavers cutting wood to build dams. A dam doesn't necessarily stop the flow of the water but it can slow it down so much until you wonder it has stopped all together. When the bowels of mercy and compassion are not moving in our relationships with each other it could be that we've dammed the river of life up with logs of bitterness, strife, unrealistic expectations, unforgiveness, and pride. At this point we're blinded by selfishness and abusive behavior has begun.

Chapter Seven
The Battered Woman

Domestic abuse is at an all time high in our country. As I sit here at my home tonight watching CNN's Larry King interview ministers and psychologists in regard to why Chris Brown physically abused Rihanna, the first thing that came to my mind was how horrible it is for a woman to be beat on by a man, and especially the man who is supposed to protect you. My mind then shifted to the abuse that God's wife, the church, has suffered and continues to suffer every day. No, I don't think that there will be a forum on CNN anytime soon discussing the horrific abuse that continues to be meted out to God's wife by the religious and greedy individuals on a daily basis. All of us have our own opinions as to why men beat up on women. While all of our opinions may have some essence of validity, yet while we're trying to argue our point, the abuse continues. Wife abuse is only one of the many tragedies of sin-it's a very ugly one, but still only one of the many.

We need to do everything that we possibly can in our society to help men who abuse women. We also need to help women be safe. Please understand that there is no cure in a bottle or a needle for domestic abuse. Even when the perpetrators are imprisoned or put to death the sickness continues. I'm not a psychologist but I do know that all men come from God and all men need God. When men who don't know God abuse women I'm not really surprised, and when men who know God abuse women I'm not really that surprised either. I'm a man, and I have never hit a woman, but I'm just as capable of doing it as the worst man in the world is-lest I lose my focus and snap. I thank God that He keeps me, but at any time I allow my ego, temper, and pride overcome me I'm capable of doing anything.

Wife abuse doesn't have to run in your biological family's background in order for you to be a wife beater; it's in Adam's line. You say, "But I've been saved and redeemed, and I'll never do anything like that." Well, so have I, but there have been mightier men than I who have fallen. Men are supposed to protect women, so why do some men choose to knock them around? Men abuse women for the same reason they abuse children, drugs, alcohol, and anything else you can think of-they abuse themselves. Why do men abuse themselves? Now I know that a man with a pocketful of money, a big house, and a two-hundred thousand dollar car appears to be anything else but abused, but abuse doesn't have to look best up and bloody in order to be called abuse. Here's the bottom line: when a man doesn't know his God he abuses himself because he abuses his purpose for being on the planet.

If a man abuses himself then he'll also abuse you. Men who don't know God don't know who they are. A man who has no identity has no affirmation. People tend to think that outward success in life means that people know who they are and have affirmation. As we all should be realizing today, nothing could be farther from the truth. Going to church does not guarantee you of your identity. People use church, money, cars, titles, positions, fortune, and fame in order to try and convince themselves and others that they know who they are, but all that stuff gradually loses its luster and the real you continue to ache.

No Quick Fix for Abusers

Wife abusers are going to need more than therapy, imprisonment, spiritual counseling, and even prayer in order for people to feel safe around them again; they're going to need God, their identity in God, affirmation, and two or three affirmed men to whom they must make themselves accountable. Until men allow the mind of Christ to be in them and to rule their thinking there are going to be continued fights between men and women, and women will suffer most of the hurt. Men who beat women don't have a childlike, kingdomgarten spirit, and most of them probably don't understand why they're like they are. But if they're willing to commit themselves and make themselves accountable to some godly authorities in their lives, they will likely bounce back and forth in their problems. One or two counseling sessions will not fix most of the severe cases of wife and child abuse evident in this country.

Going forward to the altar during Sunday's service is okay, but it's not the final answer either. A woman who has been beat by a man will perhaps wonder if he'll do it again. If a man who has abused a woman is anxious to get back with her and has not given himself to talking, walking, studying, fasting, and praying with other men, then I would advise that woman so say, "No!"

Stop Beating God's Wife!

I know that this has to break God's heart because He has chosen the woman to be an example of His church and just like women throughout this country are being violated every day and so is God's wife. The bride of Christ has black eyes, busted eardrums, broken teeth, a dislocated jaw, and is bleeding internally.

The woman with the issue of blood is a picture of the church even to this very day. She has spent all of her money. What did she do with it? She gave it to the doctors (we call them preachers today). How long has she been bleeding inside? For twelve years. Twelve is the number that represents foundation. She's been in the church long enough now to be walking in foundational truth. Why isn't she walking in foundational truth? Well, she was just a member of the congregation and had no position or title. She came to church every time the doors opened and clapped and sang and shouted amen, but all she ever saw was the back of someone else's head. The doctors preach and go home and the same thing happens each time. The leaders don't relate to each other or to the people. There is no bone to His bone connection. Every meeting is just like the previous one; the saints are reminded of how badly they've failed God, or just as worse how good they are and have no need of repentance. This woman gets beat up every week and keeps showing up for more. We often ask why men hit women, but the real mind boggler is why women keep come back for more.

All men, saved or unsaved, are certainly capable of abusing a woman, so if you're a woman and you've already seen Joe Willie's temper, get him some help now, and if he accepts it then fine, but if he doesn't then don't marry him. Get away from him. Down through the years some of the most dogged out women I've seen were women in the church. This abuse of women in the church was symbolic of the abuse being done to the church. Many women were abused either by their husbands or by others in the church. The main reason that abuse occurs is because people don't know and appreciate the purpose of people and things. Many people are sick, know they're sick, and are not looking to be healed. They're addicted to being sick. If you join a sick church you'll more than likely get sick also.

When you become addicted to someone else's addiction the disease is called codependency. When you become a codependent you just keep coming back for more abuse. Even when you know you're going to get a beating you show up right on time. People, who were codependents before they received official leadership titles and positions, unless they get delivered, will more than likely suppress others who sit under them, thus making codependents of them. This may not be the only reason why men beat up on God's wife, but it for sure is a pretty obvious one. I'm not a clinician or a psychologist but I know abuse when I see it. I also recognize insecurity, control and manipulation, and ruthlessness. Like the woman with the issue of blood who finally mustered up enough courage to say, "I'm going to Jesus, and if I can just touch the hem of His garment I'll be made whole", I've had to look deeply into my own life for signs or symptoms of anything that could be detrimental to another person's mental, physical, or spiritual well-being.

Jesus Love His Wife!

We must fully understand that Jesus love His wife. He nourishes and cares for her. He beautifies and sanctifies her. She is the only thing in all of creation that He has ever bought; He purchased her with His own blood (Acts 20:28). His wife lives in every place where there are people. Even if they aren't redeemed they were deemed to be His. This is why He gave gifts "for" men, all men, including the rebellious (Psalms 68:18). The whole purpose of God giving gifts to the church was so that He could be with His people.

The woman at the well, (another type of the church) had worship pinned down to a geographical location in Jerusalem, and Jesus had to help her see where and what true worship was (John 4:7-29). Today there are still so many wife beaters who don't know where the real Jerusalem is. The New Jerusalem, the church of the living God, the bride of Christ, is not a physical piece of land in the Middle East. The redeemed are the land, the city not forsaken, the place He went away to prepare, the Israel of God- we are His land, and He's in the middle of us. Men are abusing people as they try to build God's church, but Jesus said that He would build His own church. This graven image that we call church today is the result of men cutting and pasting bits and pieces from this place and that place and then calling it church. That's not church, that's a crossword puzzle! When anyone sews a garment without a pattern they can call it whatever they like. This explains why there are nearly three thousand religious organizations, denominations, or affiliations that all answer to the name of "church" today.

God revealed the pattern for church to Moses in the old book (Exodus) and to the apostles and the elders in the new book.

If what we call church today is the result of following the pattern that Christ laid out for us, then we have a mixed up husband. But we have a husband who died for us so we can be assured that He would never abuse us, so if there's abuse it has to come from men who think they know what the pattern is. We abuse His wife because we are trained to follow the traditions of those who were before us. Like King Saul of old we never once inquire as to where God is. We abuse His bride because we're afraid to change. It's much easier to just keep doing what we've been doing, and now we're abusing His bride because we're insane. The church is not "common" or unclean(Acts 10:14-15); it is a dedicated thing, holy unto the Lord, so when men take what is devoted to God and use it for their own self serving interest-God will intervene. Men are busy working doing their own thing while God is at rest from all of His works. If God hasn't shown you to do it then it's coming down.

Unholy Hookups

How can a woman be happy with a man that God has told her not to hook up with? How can a man find peace with a woman that God has said to walk on by? Men just don't have time to hear God today. People are being run through church services today faster than car parts in an assembly line. People are living together, not married, but greedy preachers don't care because all they want is money and a warm pew. So what if you're gay! We'll just let you sing, or play, because we really need your anointed skill. Abusers don't care about the souls of people- but only what they can get out of them.

When men don't get rid of their personal demons people with familiar spirits will attach themselves to them and adulterous, sinful, and wicked motivations will become their new company of friends. A moral weakling in the pulpit will produce a disaster in the pews. When abuse like this persists men can't really follow God and what results is one program after another. Men's day, women's day usher day, choir day children's day, founder's day, mother's day father's day, Easter day ,Christmas Day, and all the other inexhaustible list of stuff to do just because somebody wants to have a program. Now I know I just killed a lot of your favorite stuff, so let me say that there's nothing wrong with none of the programs I named, but the problem is this: What if God wants to do something else? And what if He's already told us to do something else ten years ago, but we didn't hear Him?

Chapter Eight
God's Authority Must be Coordinated

L eadership must lead and know what God's pattern is and then coordinate God's authority among the saints. We abuse God's people whenever we fail to coordinate His authority within the body of His people. Whether it's in the home, the church, the business world, the federal government, the NFL, the NBA, baseball, hockey, or Hollywood, all authority comes from God and is delegated to men who in turn must coordinate it. Our world is full of abuse because men do not submit to God's authority. The church was created by God to demonstrate His love to the whole world. Problems occur whenever those under this covenant refuse to submit to God and to one another. Church is a joke in the minds of many people for the simple fact that a lot of people who claim to be Christians behave like the devil. The devil is the one who introduced abuse and rebellion to the earth.

Adam abused his wife by not speaking the Word of the Lord. Adam's abuse, which was neglect, was passed on to all of mankind. If a man neglects his wife she'll move miles ahead of him. Women will move, and it doesn't take a rocket scientist to figure this out. This is the very reason why there's so much abuse being done to God's wife. Men must wake up from all the lies of the past and from all the labels that society and culture have pinned on them. God makes no distinction between men on the basis of color or race.

If God can get a man, and I mean any man, to conform to the culture of His kingdom, then He'll use that man to do His bidding. Society says that men are non communicators, but that's a lie because men were born to initiate God's delegated authority. As long as men stay ignorant of what God says about them they'll always be abusive in some shape or fashion. A man must study the woman he's married to. He must also understand that God has put him in the position of priest of the home, and that the "man"-tle of leadership rests upon him. He doesn't have to be as vocal, or as smart as his wife—he just needs to know who his Father is and who he is in Him. If he does not love his wife like Christ loved the church, then he has already abused her. If a man gets married and is not capable of leading about a wife, depending on the nature of the woman he's married to, all hell could break out. Abuse is inevitable.

There's neither male or female

The truth of the matter is that both male and female make up the body of Christ. When the bible says that there's neither male nor female in Christ (Galatians 3:28), it's not referring to the composition of the Lord's body but to the essence of our relationship with Christ. There's no division in the Lord's body. In a marriage the man and the woman are one. The male has a functional role and the female has a functional role. Cleaning house, washing dishes, teaching the kids, cooking meals are tasks that both sexes can do, but a male is just not equipped and blessed by God to be able to get pregnant and have a baby. When a male want to change his body and be able to have a baby, that's called "confusion", and when a woman decides that she's a male (regardless of her reason) that's confusion as well. Now, men have abused women for centuries in the church.

I know preachers who have told women that they couldn't teach, preach, or even come up behind the pulpit. I also know many women who need to get from behind the pulpit, stop preaching, teaching, prophesying, and go back home and start love on their husbands. Now, since there's neither male nor female in Christ, men are also candidates for abuse. There are many men who suffer abuse every time the church doors open. A man has no business taking a woman in marriage that is not capable of following his godly lead, but it's far too late to say this for some because the church is loaded with such couples. If a woman, and I don't care how fine she is, or how much money she has, does not know what it means to reverence and respect her man (saved or unsaved), then he should leave her with her father. The church is filled with people both young and old who came from homes where fathers were abusive to mothers, and mothers ran their mouths like an automatic rifle. This cycle of family dysfunctionalism goes on in the church and in society from generation to generation. So abuse becomes generational. God's wife has been beaten for generations. The reason why the abuse continues is men often repent unto salvation and start following God in principle, but never repent unto the kingdom of God and follow Him in practice. It's easy to confess that you love the Lord, but it requires true conversion to follow Him in practical living.

It's easy to stand at an altar and vow to love your wife like Christ loved the church, but when she starts breathing out flames like the dragon from hell, you immediately say, "This isn't the woman I married!" It's tough for two people to live together in peace. Now if you just multiply this factor by two or three hundred people, and put them all under one roof, now you can see why men keep beating up on God's wife. When believers fight each other they do harm to the body of Christ, which is one. If a man does harm to his wife he does harm to himself as well. There's no excuse for abuse of any kind among covenant people. The reason it goes on and on is because men won't do what Jesus says. Jesus said that His kingdom was not of this world, if it were then would His servants fight (John). Men fight in the church and abuse each other because they refuse to get converted and become as little children (Matthew: 1-4).

Don't abuse one another—but do fight!

The believer's fight, and one and only fight, must be the good fight of faith (1 Tim. 6:12). Our fight must never be over meat and drink issues such as race, color, titles, positions, hearsay, money, possessions, doctrines, or any of the number of "little foxes" that that divide people. Our only hope for success is to enter the kingdom of heaven. If you like fighting and violence I offer you this solution: "The kingdom of heaven suffers violence but the violent take it by force" (Matthew 11:12). The type of violence that is required to enter the kingdom of heaven is not the kind that is exacted against other people, but it is your earnest decision to lay aside anything and everything that hinders the rule and reign of God in your life. And this requires a violent action on our part. Violence comes from the Greek word "bios", which refers to life, or living. A. violent man seizes or takes things from others. So a violent believer takes or seizes his life from the spirit of religion and yields it to the rightful owner, Jesus.

We live in a very violent world. Trouble or tribulations are all around us, but it is through much tribulation that we must enter the kingdom of God. Adults tend to magnify trouble and thus live in fear, but children don't seem to be bothered that much by it. Children wake up excited everyday looking forward to meal time, snack time show and tell time, and play time. When it's time for bed many children pitch a fit. Parents can be so poor that they can hardly pay attention but their children think that "money grows on tree." Hey', don't be too critical of children for thinking that money grows on trees, and realistically we know it doesn't, but since our heavenly Father owns the cattle on a thousand hills, as well as all the silver and the gold, maybe we would do better by becoming "as" little children and start calling the things that be not as though they were. Men of understanding know that money doesn't grow on trees, but that money comes from trees. Jesus gives two powerful keys about entering the kingdom in Matthew 18:1-4 when He talks about conversion, and then "becoming as a little child."

Conversion, Coordination, and the Kingdom

Face it, all we have to work with is men and women. In our unredeemed and unholy minds God doesn't expect us to do anything but abuse each other. But He knows that the Holy Ghost can teach us all things. He knows that if we give ourselves to the process of conversion, we'll coordinate His delegated authority in the home and in His church, and His mighty kingdom will come in our settings. Conversion obviously refers to the new birth, or being born again. It means to change something from one state to a different state. Water is changed to ice by lowering the temperature, and ice changes to water as the temperature is raised. Sinners are converted from the state of sin to the state of righteousness. In Christ we've become "new creatures", or a new creation, because old things are passed away and all things are new and are of God (2Corinthians 5:17).Old things passing away, all things becoming new, and all things being of God ,suggests that there are "things" we must embrace during the process.

The key to conversion is the expression "being in Christ". This is more than saying the sinner's prayer and joining a church. People do this all the time. The emphasis is on Christ, or being in Christ, because the bible states that "in Him" we live, move, and has our being. So it's not simply, in Christ, but it's if any man "be" in Christ. There are three dimensions of knowing Christ listed in Acts 17:28- there's living, there's moving, and then there's having our being. "Being" in Christ is the greatest of the three; it's the third dimension. Ice doesn't just melt all at once. It breaks down in a "process" gradually. Now you can slow down the process or you can speed it up, but it's still nonetheless a process. Water also freezes through a process. Oh how some people just absolutely hate process?

That's why many people join a geographical building we call church, but don't join Jesus. And this further explains why some Christians are either as cold as ice, or as unstable as water. God doesn't do process. He does the end right from the beginning. He completes us in Christ and sticks us in time, and in time we must either freeze or thaw out. You can either spend your entire life doing, doing, doing, or you can transcend time and start being who He called you to be. Remember, I talked about "being" caught up, or raptured away in a previous chapter.

When you have the mind of Christ it allows you to think on things above, and not on things beneath. Above is where Christ is seated, and it's also where you are "seated" with Him. It's not simply looking up toward a mountain or at the sky, but it's a change in mind-set or dimensions. He has made us the head, and never the tail, above only, and never beneath. Your greatest struggle is between your ears, because this is where anti-Christ sets up his shop in the temple of God and your body is the temple of the living God. Don't confine the anti-Christ to some far away region in the Middle East, that's exactly what he wants you to do, because now he can reign in your "middle", that is between your ears. In God's economy a mind's not a terrible thing to waste, no, no; the old mind is a good thing to get rid of. Your old mind is disgusting and dirty. It wants to run up and down every prostituted alley, every filthy avenue, and commit the vilest of sins. Stop trying to make it better and get rid of it.

Jesus said to become converted and then become "as", and not become little children. He also said to Peter that when you are converted, or fully converted, I want you to strengthen your brothers. Peter, like many people today, assumed he'd been converted, got the opportunity to experience his carnal mind taking the lead in his walk with the Lord. You can't become a kingdomgarten kid until you've been converted and become as a little child. You don't sit down and decide that in two years I'm going to be converted, and then in six months I'll be a kingdomgarten kid. I know that we live in the microwave age, but don't be "childish" and try to microwave your spiritual growth. God knows just how long to keep you in the furnace and at what temperature to set the furnace. Time belongs to God. God is not bound by time because God is Spirit and He lives in eternity.

God has set chronos (clock and calendar time) into motion and it moves whether you move or not. But kairos time is time in the spirit, and even when you're sleep it's moving, but if your mind is carnal you're denied entry. Clock time is conscious time, while kairos time is not counting the seconds, and even though they're moving, your consciousness is elsewhere. You're not "self-conscious". Children having fun and are completely oblivious to things around them are caught away in kairos time. Have you heard the expression," time flies when you're having fun?" Well, you don't count time in the spirit. My point is that people who give themselves to the spirit are not going to be the people who are constantly fussing and bickering about time related issues. All you had to do to experience chronos time is cry when the doctor spanked you, but you'll never become the person God intended you to become unless you make a "definite" response to God's announcement of kairos time. When Jesus showed up and said, or announced, "The kingdom of heaven is at hand", He was saying that the kairos of God has come to you, God has come to you, heaven has come to you, power has come to you, authority has come to you, so repent (stop thinking the way you've been thinking) and believe the gospel. Turn away from chronos and embrace kairos. People are always talking about the end of time, and whenever they do this it scares the devil out of some because they've always been so time conscious and in control of everything.

Flesh is in control in chronos time. This is the reason why Christians don't mature; don't you know that the bible says that if you live after the flesh you'll die (Romans 8:13)? However, if you'll allow the Spirit to mortify (put to death) the deeds of the flesh, you'll live. You're worried about dying and the end of time and God has already reckoned you dead in the death of His Son and given you eternal life by the resurrection of His Son. He's also given you His Spirit so that you may know that all these things are true. Learning to walk in the Spirit and be conformed to His image, or converted, is comparable to the way water freezes in the freezer. If it's in the freezer, and the freezer is working, it will freeze. It's not a matter of "if" it freezes, it's "when" it freezes. If you will then, the water is taken out of chronos and placed in kairos. The water is in the spirit. So then, if you walk, or live, in the Spirit, you will not fulfill the lusts of the flesh. Many people confuse this scripture (Galatians 5:16) and turn the order around and start trying as hard as they can to not fulfill the lusts of the flesh in hopes that they'll walk in the Spirit, but it doesn't work in that order. Remember, walk in the Spirit, or put the water in the operable freezer, and you will not fulfill the lusts of the flesh, and you will have ice for the party. The refrigerator and the Spirit do the work, and not you and the water. The Spirit does the work of conversion in a person's life, but the time factor is determined by the how well your refrigerator works, or if it works at all. Are you cooperating with God?

Chapter Nine
Put First Things First

Now, first things must always come first. If church wasn't necessary then God wouldn't have given it to us. The fact that men abuse the glorious purpose of church is their own business. Jesus came to introduce the kingdom, not church. Adam's wife came from his side, and Jesus' wife came from His side also. The church and the kingdom are not the same thing. Men are born, or reborn, into the church, but must choose to enter the kingdom. Men can remain proud and grown up all of their lives in church, but unless they get converted and become as little children they will never enter the kingdom.

The church is the "ekklesia", the called out ones, and the kingdom is within the called out ones. We are the church, but God gives us the kingdom. Everything in the kingdom is in the church, but not everything that's in the church is in the kingdom.

Jesus told a church man named Nicodemus that if he wasn't born again he would never see the kingdom of God. For all practical purposes Nicodemus was already a believer in Jesus and was part of the church, but the problem was he had never repented to the kingdom of God. Remember, Jesus said to the people of His day, "repent, for the Kingdom of heaven is at hand!" Since it's the Father's good pleasure to give us the kingdom, it now becomes our decision to accelerate or decelerate; it's in our hand. You're in the car and you're driving, so what are you going to do? Speed up; slow down, stop, or what? I know that the smart guys are going to say that they're going to drive the speed limit and not break the law, but this is exactly the reason why so many saints are dying at the wheel (in church)-they're just playing it safe in church. You're in the church, and now what are you going to do? Take the kingdom by force, stay where you are and rot away, or go back into the hole Jesus pulled you out of?

If I may, please allow me to use a little baseball analogy. The idea in baseball is to win the game by getting men on base and then advancing them all the way around the bases to score at home plate. This can be done by getting a walk, getting hit by a pitch, getting a base hit, hitting a home run, or stealing a base. The most horrible statistic in baseball and the one that managers and owners hate the most is LOB, which stands for men Left on Base. No true baseball player likes to put out with men left on base. The reason you're in the lineup is to get on base, or move the runners ahead that are already on base; that is your purpose.

Church and Kingdom

The church serves a glorious purpose because it ushers people into the kingdom of God. If you're a believer you don't have to look far or long for the kingdom because it's the Father's good pleasure to give it to you (Luke 12:32). There's a language, a lifestyle, and a culture of the kingdom that God has hidden from the wise and prudent and has revealed to everyone who is willing to become as little children and believe that their Father will supply their each and every need. It's really sad because so many saints are locked securely inside the walls of the church and don't even know that the kingdom exists. It's not God or the Bible that holds them there, but it's their denominational dogmas and doctrines that they insist upon keeping. Many of these sweet and loving saints will die and go to heaven never knowing what their purpose was for living.

I know people right now, and some are dear friends of mine, who have been in church all of their lives but are trapped by their own doctrine. They have their own private interpretation of the scriptures. They hold sins against people who have been divorced or remarried. At first they may be real friendly toward new people, but the minute they find out that you've been divorced or married to someone who was divorced, the chill is on. In their eyes you are an adulterer, and you are hell bound! God will forgive you but you must punish yourself by living alone for the rest of your life. If we were kingdomgarten kids we wouldn't have made such a big mess out of the issue of marriage, divorce, and remarriage.

Many men and women in the church who choose not to be married are driven into homosexual lifestyles by people who tell them that they're weird for not being married. There are still those among us who will never receive marriage as their gift. These people are able to contain themselves. They don't lay awake at night burning with the desire to have sex. When religious minded church folk insist that everybody gets married they may not realize it but they're actually saying that God made all men and women the "same", and that there's no such thing as eunuchs form birth, as well as people who choose never to be married. This gross ignorance of the word of God on the part of people is just as much a "homosexual" mind set as is the actual lifestyle that some people choose to live.

It's an abomination for men to sleep with men and women to sleep with women, but it's just as much an abomination for churches to fall in love with doctrines that have nothing to do with God, and also insist that these doctrines be practiced by all who follow in years and generations to come. Two men or two women in a sexual relationship with one another may have themselves a jolly old good time but that's about all that'll come to past, because God never intended for this type relationship to exist; at the same time any church that falls in love with a doctrine or a tradition that insists that everyone wear the same clothes, eat the same foods, vote for the same political candidate, or even interpret scriptures the same way–is really trying to make everyone the "same", which is "homosexual".

What I'm about to say now is something you may not like, so be warned if you keep reading. Any church that is run by "all men", or by "all women", is out of order and needs to seek God for instructions. Any "all male" or "all female" leadership that vehemently opposes the involvement of the opposite sex is in danger of producing a homosexual body. Since every seed reproduces after its own kind, don't be surprised when people of the same gender start burning with desire for others of the same sex. Those who attend college, or plan to, had best be warned about the possible deception hidden in the lives and agendas of many people involved in sororities and fraternities. No, gay and lesbian lifestyles is definitely not even mentioned in any of their literature, but neither was there a sign posted at the gate entering Sodom and Gomorrah that read, "Welcome Gays," Of course you don't have to pledge a sorority or a fraternity to be introduced to homosexuality, because it certainly exists in the general population and in many cases among the faculty and staff as well. My point is that God never intended for any type perversion to exist among His body, the church. However, the church has to deal with sexual perversion because leaders who don't know who they are pass their nasty disease on to others who don't know who they are.

The church was supposed to manifest a picture of the perfectly balanced relationships between men and women, however she has failed terribly. I don't know if you've noticed it or not but there is an obvious aggressive sexually driven revolution by the female gender today. Older women, especially high-profile women, and teenage girls, seem to have a very sensuous desire for flesh of the same gender as well as younger men. Older female movie starlets who today call themselves "cougars", a predatory animal, are thirsty for the flesh men young enough to be their sons and grandsons. Young women can be seen at parties and on dance floors clutching and grinding each other as they dance with one another. Masculinity is at an all-time low. The church is manifesting all sorts of perversion- punks in the pulpit, perverts and child molesters in the children's ministry, and men who have grown tired of their own wives and now are dating other men, yet pasturing at the same time.

Come to order Men!

Are you offended because I've put the church and the male of the species at the fore front of responsibility? It may not be your fault sir, but it most surely is your responsibility. No, it's not your fault when your child cuts up at school, but it most certainly is your responsibility to bring correction and discipline to your child, isn't it? The whole world is out of order because man, the male of the species, is out of order. Those men and women in our world who are driven by impure desires for strange flesh are happy and excited because men are out of order because it allows them more opportunities to fulfill their inordinate desires and lusts. When the strong man is bound the goods in the house are spoiled.

I read an article in Charisma recently that referred to Oprah's false gospel, and that she (Oprah) is the "unofficial" high priestess of America's new morality. Well if you want to give Oprah that kind of credit go right ahead and have at it, but how could any of us with our heads above the ground in this hour not plainly see that the "official" high priestess of America's immorality is the "make believe" church? No, don't panic, I love the church, that is, the church that Jesus purchased with His own blood, and the one that is that has yielded to Him as He continues to build her. Sure, the true bride has problems too, but there's also real and true accountability present so that problems can be dealt with from within, rather than aired out on the national media. God has never told His people, and He never will, to debate whether or not homosexuality, or any other iniquity, is a sinful condition that can be overcome by His grace. God has never instructed His church to sit in forums and argue over anything. The church has not been called to debate, but to demonstrate. The mere fact that we use the word "issue" to talk about things that should be clear to us as Christians suggest that we're confused, and are in need of help ourselves.

People argue and debate because they're not totally convinced that something is true. There are a few things that we could possibly sit down and discuss, but homosexuality is surely not one. God loves all men but He hates all sin. There's no platform to discuss the wrath of God that has been revealed form heaven against all ungodliness of men who hold the truth of God in unrighteousness. We need to stop this wavering back and forth like the waves of the ocean. God has not called His people to be "double-minded" I believe that when Jesus spoke about two men being in one bed He was really referring to a double-minded man, or a man who was unstable in all his ways, and not necessarily two men in an effeminate relationship.

If you believe that God created mankind to function in this life as either male or female then why are you entertaining the possibility of a third gender? A male trying to function as a female is perversion. A female trying to function as a male is also perversion. Among believers there was never to be any confusion concerning a person's sexuality. When non-believers overhear so-called Christians stumbling furiously trying to answer questions of this nature all it does is produce more doubt and confusion in their minds. Christians are supposed to have compassion on the lost, and not make themselves look stupid trying to answer questions that gender strife and go on and on forever. If you know God then go ahead and glorify Him as God, or else start your own talk show.

The best time to teach and affirm people about their sexuality is during the kindergarten years of their lives. Unfortunately it is during these precious and tender years that many young children are defiled. It was and still is God's plan for children to be protected during these years, but there are so many who don't fear God nor keep His commandments.

Visual Learners

The colors of the American flag are red, white, and blue, and these is crystal clear, so why would you stand there and go on and on with someone who tells you that that's not really red, white or blue, but the flag is solid green? Whenever good is called evil, and evil is called good, confusion fills the air. The problem in religion is that we've tried to tell the lost world, by using enticing words of men's wisdom that Jesus Christ's amazing grace has the power to transform people, but it's a lot easier process when you're able to present a clear visual of what you're trying to present. Oh I know that there have been numerous examples but the world always goes to pot for the lack of the next good example. No matter how aged or spiritually mature we become, we, all of us, are still tactile, kinesthetic learners. Our children hear the words that are coming out of our mouths, but they're anxiously waiting for the lights, camera, and action to begin. Oprah makes her living by talking to people, and if I remember correctly it's called a "talk show", so if you're ever invited to appear on a talk show make sure you carry a good and "clear picture "with you.

Dropouts

In his speech to the joint session of congress on February 24, 2009 President Barack Obama stated that education is a prerequisite in turning things around in America. He went on to say that the United States has one of the highest dropout rates of any industrialized nation in the world. According to President Obama there are no substitutes for a mom and a dad in the home, and that we must not pass on to our children debt they cannot pay.

I've included no data or statistics in my book for the simple reason that if only one child has dropped out of school it is far too many. Besides, facts and figures simply bore most people anyway. Do you remember when you first heard the slogan, "no child left behind?" I certainly do, and I thought, what in the world were we supposed to be doing all the time? Do you mean that in the classrooms across America we actually had teachers who were literally holding children back and didn't want them to be successful? I always wanted every child I taught to learn and pass. When a child failed a test I gave I would always think about what I could have done differently to help the child have success. I don't believe that teachers are the reason that children dropout of school, but at the same time I do believe that a teacher can be the main reason a child stays in school. Moms and Dads may have forsaken their children, so now the teacher stands in proxy for the parents. Heck, in many situations the teacher is the parent.

Children go to school five days a week for about eight hours a day, which totals to forty hours a week. Most children sleep for about eight hours a night, which totals to fifty six hours a week. If parents are at work during the night they don't see their children a whole lot. And God forbid that parents have to work on weekends. The average teacher in America actually spends more time with children than the parents do. So if a child drops out of school please don't let it be your fault teacher. For the most part children love school. They love seeing their friends and interacting with them. They probably don't like every class or subject but there's at least one teacher or one class that every child looks forward to. When a child doesn't connect to another child, or teacher, and has a horrible home life that child becomes a candidate for dropping out. We can readily spot the children on the streets that have dropped out of school because they're getting in trouble and causing problems, but what about the dropouts who show up every day for school yet have connected with no one. The good news they're in school and accounted for, but the bad news is they're non-existent in their own minds-hopefully not yours. When children start to feel that no one cares about them they overcome the sense of worthlessness. Their dreams of becoming a doctor, a lawyer, a teacher, an engineer, an athlete, a soldier, a pilot, or an artist is not all together crushed but is so deeply suppressed beneath hard words and neglect of others until just getting out of bed every day is a struggle.

Most children who drop out of school don't just all of a sudden one day decide to quit, but they are slowly eliminated by a cold and callous system that has very little regard for who they are and what they can become. Many people think that children from what I call "the hood" drop out of school in order to sell drugs. I totally disagree with this hare-brained notion. I believe children are on the streets selling drugs because they're not in school. They didn't quit school to sell drugs, but they're selling drugs because they quit school. And besides that, maybe the drug dealer showed them more attention than the people who were supposed to be helping them did. Children who come from a dysfunctional home where adults fuss, argue, and fight all the time have become conditioned to chaos, and are not accustomed to order and structure that teachers demand, consequently they tend to act out in such settings. Without wise intervention they'll drop out because all they do is start trouble.

A great number of school drop outs are what I consider to be average students. Average kids will "drop through the crack" in schools where teachers and counselors spend all their time with the college bound and the disruptive children. If a school wants to raise its test scores the smart thing to do is make sure that students who fall in the middle group receive more help than the other two groups of students. I really don't like what's happened in public schools in regards to testing. It seems that our schools have become "testing centers" rather than "learning centers." This was not by design I'm sure, but has come about as a result of the serious breakdown in family life. Daddy is either working two jobs, or he's on drugs or gambling, dead, or in jail. Mommy, or granny in many cases, is so stressed with the magnitude of what she's up against until she has to drink or pop pills just to cope. Need I not mention the great number of babies who are trying to raise babies on their own? I won't even bother to address the vast number of school systems with classroom teachers who start teaching just because they thought it was a good idea. Hats off to all the parents, teachers, administrators, and community workers who get up every day with helping children on their minds and retire every night doing the same-you're beautiful!

Parental Involvement

From my own personal observations as a former elementary school teacher and also principal, I have watched the gradual decline of parental involvement in the lives of children from pre-k through fifth grade. The school meetings for pre-k through first grade for parents were greater in attendance than those of second through fifth grade. If you think that your child needs you less as he matriculates through the educational process you're nuts. This "hands off" approach with children as they move from one grade to another is certainly a catalyst in the dropout rate. Parental involvement at the elementary level is poor, is almost non-existent at the middle school level, and "you're on your own" at the high school level. And you wonder why children drop out of school? During the elementary years children will hold their parents hands and tell them how much they love them, during the middle school years boys don't want to be seen dead with their parents but parents can't be intimidated by this bit of adolescent behavior, and when they're in high school they need you more than ever. Oh how they need parents in high school, because everything that you ever taught them is suddenly put on trial for its life as they deal with their own identity, their sexuality, fitting in, and the possibility of leaving home for the first time. Parents who don't realize this are forcing their children to drop out. Our world is at an all time high when it comes to the age at which people have kids.

Parents who had children when they were mere teens are usually with their children when they're real small, but as their children start growing up these same parents spend less time with them because they try to catch up on all the fun they missed from having kids so early. Many children drop out because they had a parent who dropped out. This curse just goes on and on and becomes the "generation curse" until somebody in the family gets hold of God and refuses to let go.

Church Dropouts

Now I know you're saying what in the world does school dropouts have to do with kingdomgarten kids in the church? Well, I thought you'd never ask if memory serves me correct the church congregation is made up of people, and not people from Mars or Venus, but people from every type home you can imagine. Highly educated people, illiterate people, middle class and blue collar workers, retired and semi-retired people, people on welfare, people who receive a crazy check, people who are trying to get a crazy check, and yes Bay Bay's kids and Bart Simpson's kids are there too. So if our country's schools are experiencing dropouts, think it not strange that the church will experience dropouts as well. There's only one church, or one body of Christ for all who follow Jesus, but people drop out of one local church and drop in to another one all the time. Some of the reasons that people drop out of church are the same as the reasons that people drop out of schools. The feeling that nobody cares about them, a dysfunctional home life, people outside the church show the more attention than people inside the church, they want to be in charge, or I just don't fit in here are just a few reasons that people drop out of church.

Someone once told me that people leave church for two reasons- you either use the too much, or you don't use them at all. There's probably a lot of truth behind that. A lot of people move from one church to another church (and I call this spiritual recycling) looking for the "fire." What fire you might ask? You know, the spectacular, the excitement, the feel good stuff, the folks falling out in the spirit kind of stuff. They're looking for the signs wonders, but they don't realize that they're the sign, and it's a wonder they don't go nuts looking for the signs and wonders. Most kids that drop out of schools never return, but church dropouts just move from church to church. A few church dropouts stay at home and watch Christian television and send money to help it continue. There are an increasing number of church dropouts who have started their own ministries, or church for fellow dropouts. They're praying that you'll "drop in" sometimes. Like many school dropouts who have gotten their GED and have become very successful, there are also many church dropouts who have given themselves lofty titles and actually have people following them. To tell the truth it may not be a bad thing for people to drop out of most of what we refer to as church, but I pray that no one drops out of the church that Jesus is building. Most of what people call church is an oppressive system set up by men. Most homes also have the same oppressive system. You mean you don't see this? It's as plain as the nose on your face. I mean no offense to any church, or to any person, but if by now in your life you're still able to be offended, then perhaps you need to be offended.

We're witnessing the destruction of children because too many of the wrong people are having children. We're watching people hop all over the place in churches because too many of the wrong people are in charge in churches. People should consult with God, who is the owner, before they marry the wrong person and have children. However, more important than "marrying" the right person is "being" the right person. Before you run off and start your own church you need to check with Jesus, because He said He would build His own church. When you start your church without Jesus' say so, all you have is "your" church. Any church or organization that does not have God's order and coordinated authority at its foundation will surely manifest an oppressive environment.

Oppression is the result of having boy leaders. Men become too lazy to mature and too proud to humble themselves and become "as" little children, Kingdomgarten kids. It's the rejection of God's word. Let me show you what happens when men reject the Word of God. God has an order for how life is supposed to go. He gives a man, then He gives a woman, they both have to know Him, they have sex only after they're married, they have children only after they're married, and they raise their children up to know Him. People have surely messed this order up, haven't they? Now, the same people who have messed God's plan for life up go and start churches. Men who don't love God or other people start churches. Men who sleep with other men start churches. Women who sleep with other women start churches. Men who have outside children that they flat out deny go and start churches. Men with cocaine addictions go and accept pastorates. People who have no clue as to who God is or who they are, go and start churches. In the book of Isaiah chapter three, the prophet speaks: "For behold, the Lord, the Lord of hosts, doth take away from Jerusalem and from Judah the stay and the staff, the whole stay of bread, and the whole stay of water. The mighty man and the man of war, the judge, and the prophet, and the prudent, and the ancient. The captain of fifty, the honorable man, the counselor, the cunning artificer, and the eloquent orator. And I will give children to be their princes, and babes shall rule over them. And the people shall be oppressed, everyone by another, and every one by his neighbor: the child shall behave himself proudly against the ancient and the base against the honorable". If after reading this you don't immediately see America's homes, schools, and churches then your coffee is cold.

We're oppressed and suffering in our society today because we don't have God's supply of godly parents, teachers, and leaders. We have plenty of food and drink but we're lacking God's supply of spiritual nourishment in the form of people. A baby needs a mother's milk and a mother's love. A young boy needs a father's love, guidance, and affirmation. A student in school needs a teacher's knowledge and patience during the learning process. What makes you think that people in churches don't need the same things? When leaders don't lead in the way of the Lord, oppression will be the result. In the absence of a true vision from the Lord people will cast off restraint, every man will seek to do what is right in his own eyes, in short, the people will perish. Your child drops out of your home because he doesn't want to follow your rules, or he wants to establish his own. This is the case of a rebellious child. But if your child drops out of your home and you didn't live by the very rules you tried to enforce on him, then this is the case of a rebellious parent. When two people live in the same house and they are both are right in their "own eyes", the result will always be oppression. The only way to avoid an environment of oppression is to have God as your Lord and King, a meek and humble delegated authority under Him,(a father, a mother, a teacher, a supervisor,etc.) and people who "willingly and obediently" connect to that delegated authority.

Every home has to have a vision. Every school must have a vision. Every business has to have a vision. Every local church of Jesus must absolutely have its own autonomous vision. We must never attempt to exercise control over a local church from a denominational headquarters. People are nomadic (Cain like), and will forever drop in and drop out, but if there's a God given clear vision in the house, they can decide real quick if this is the place for them or not. A vision for a local church is the God given mandate written in the heart of the visionary, and then written on tablets for all who are to follow. It's everything that a particular people are to do and become. The vision is the picture that everyone in the house must look to and submit to. The vision is living and spiritual thing. If the vision in the local church is written and made plain it will actually settle arguments and disputes among the people submitted to it. A goal is something that you want to accomplish, but the vision is what keeps you in line as you accomplish the goal.

Many times the goals and projects that an organization wants to accomplish end up in chaos and confusion because there is no true vision that unites people and gives them direction. In the church the vision must come from the Lord. No local church should ever accept or follow the vision of a headquarters control group or board. God has given the church its mission, or its great commission, and that is the same for the entire church, but the manner in which the mission is carried out is determined by the unique vision given to the leader. Without a true vision from the Lord the best a body of people can do is what another church is doing. The vision is not just words on paper, but it's seeing it in your heart and running with it, or adapting your lifestyle to it. The vision pertains to what God wants to do with your life. It pertains to your purpose and your destiny. Every person on earth was created to accomplish certain things while on earth. But every person is also to become conformed to the image of God's Son. Every local church is located in a particular geographical setting and is supposed to do a particular work in its setting. Every person in a local church setting has their own individual purpose and vision for their life, and must now submit everything to the greater vision of the house.

The things that you want to accomplish in the next three to five years are only part of the vision for your life, because everything that you want to accomplish must serve a greater purpose. For example, you want to finish your degree in two years; this is your plan, but the scriptures say that many are the plans of a man's heart, but it's God's purpose that must prevail (Proverbs19:21). In other words, if it doesn't serve God's purpose then don't do it. The couple that plans to have a child needs to ask themselves why? Why do we want a child? What will we do with a child? What will this child do in life? Who will this child become? We are experiencing widespread abuse in our world today simply because we do not know the purpose of things (children, women, drugs, alcohol, money, authority, the church, etc.).I purposely left men out of the list of things that are abused because men have been created to take the lead in the stewardship of the earth. Men actually cause all other abuses in the world by not obeying the God who created them. Know purpose and no abuse. God knows exactly what He wants every person He gives life to, to accomplish. Vision is what He shows us about what He wants us to do. A vision is not just a glorified business plan but it is a real live spiritual organism. It can be heard, seen, written, waited on, and it can also talk (Habakkuk 2: 1-3). The vision can be heard because it is an "oracle", or word, from the Lord to God's man. It can be seen because God reveals it by the Spirit. It is written on the heart of God's man. We must wait on it because it comes out of eternity into time for manifestation. It speaks because it is the word of God spoken to our heart. Remember, without a vision the people will perish, but without a people the vision will perish. Without a vision from the Lord the people will never see the kingdom, for they will stay locked up in a "churchy" mind set and do their own thing all lifelong, because only a true kingdomgarten kid can receive the vision of the Lord. Grown folk like to argue and make excuses about what they cannot do. Moses objected to every point that God made to him about telling Pharaoh to let His people go.

Grown folk have to know where every rest stop is located along the way, but all kids want to know is, "are we there yet?" Grown men run and hide when Goliath romps out and raises his booming voice, but a kingdomgarten kid just picks up five smooth stones from the stream (one rock for the giant Goliath and four more just in case kin folk want to jump in) and knocks the giant's head off. It's interesting that the "grown-up" army ran and hid from Goliath, but a kingdomgarten kid named David had a God who was bigger and badder than any giant he would ever face. When the giant said that he had been a warrior from his youth, David knew that he had been a worshipper from his youth. The warrior has to fight his own battles, but the worshipper doesn't have to fight, because God fights for him. When you fight your own battles God becomes smaller in your eyes, but when you constantly worship God He becomes larger in your eyes. King Saul missed out on the kingdomgarten of life, and consequently he knows nothing about the worship of God. Like Goliath, King Saul was also a warrior, but neither one was a worshipper. David was also a warrior, but only because he was a worshipper first. David wasn't a dropout. He took his kingdomgarten skills right on with him to the battlefield. Saul was described as a man who was in a class all by himself in his stature form his shoulders up. Saul was a head and shoulders man. David was a heart man. Experienced and loving teachers know that if they can reach a child's heart them they will not likely drop out of school. People drop out of school, church, and marriages because of heart matters.

Man's heart has to be circumcised. The "foreskin" of hatred against God must be removed. When David was facing Goliath he referred to him as an "uncircumcised Philistine" (1 Samuel). David knew that Goliath was a dropout, and that he had no covenant relationship with God, therefore The God of Israel would give him victory over his enemies. Later on in his life David would also discover that Saul was also a church dropout who never even asked anyone about the presence of God- the Ark of the Covenant. Like many people today Saul only had himself on his mind. See if you can spot yourself in this next chapter.

Chapter Ten
Users and Givers

When it comes down to human relationships everyone will fall into one or two categories.

You will either be a user or a giver. For people who insist that they don't belong to either group they must be warned that it's only a matter of time before you very strongly begin to manifest the strengths of either group. Users want everything. They remind me of the bullies I knew back in grade school. They take your lunch, your lunch money, your marbles, your homework, and even your girlfriend. The take stuff and they use it for or on themselves. Never mind about getting it back because if you try you could get beat up really bad. Somehow the users never dropped out of school; in fact they have perfect attendance. Yes, they were there every day just to make life miserable for you.

Most "old school" users got their start in grade school. The guys who took your lunch money back in grade school are now taking the welfare check from the girl who lives in the low-income subsidized housing apartment with three kids. Please, if you're a parent with small children, watch out for potential "user" behavior patterns them. The providers at our child development center are trained to redirect children who insist upon having a toy that another child is playing with. We don't allow a child to fall out on the floor kicking and screaming for a toy that another child had first. If children don't learn to share, or understand that taking turns is perfectly fine, as they grow older the user personality gets stronger. When you redirect a child you give him other options, and in this case toys, to play with. Invariably the redirected child will still want the toy that they couldn't have, but by this time the other child has likely found interest in something else. If you notice that a child just follows other children around and cries for the toys that they have then the parents need to know, if they're not already aware, about their child's behavior. Any parent or adult who allows this type behavior to persist in a child is helping to create a monster. Children must learn to share when they're very small

The consequences of not learning to share at an early age are widespread in our society today. Many parents just don't realize that high strung personality disorders in small children are just as addictive as crack cocaine. If these disorders are not corrected in a loving, firm, and diplomatic manner then the parent, or the supervising adult, actually becomes a codependent. Millions of people are addicted to their own children's addiction. I call it being used by tiny users. The sad reality is that tiny cry babies will grow up to become big time users. How many relationships that you know of right now where a family member or friend of yours is in bondage to a user's addiction? You don't have to look far to spot one, do you? The guy that won't work to provide for his family and himself is more than likely a user. The girl who suffers from lack of affirmation and identity by a father, but has learned how to use guilt and manipulation on other people in order to take care of herself and her children, is a user. I don't believe that people are born users, but I believe that we're all born with basic needs, and if our basic needs are not supplied in the proper fashion we will do whatever is convenient to have our needs met.

An individual's needs pertain to the things that are necessary to the sustaining of life. Food, water and air are necessary for physical life to continue. Safety is also a very important basic need, but users are willing to neglect the safety issue just to eat and drink. Countless numbers of small children have been left in unsafe environments by user parents and have been abused by sexual perverts, petrifies, and pornographers. Many children who survive this horrific abuse go on to become users themselves. The higher order needs like the social, emotional, and spiritual needs are also vitally important. When parents neglect the needs of their children they are setting them up to become users. Every marriage has basic needs that must be met. When husbands and wives ignore one another's needs they will often turn to someone else to fulfill their needs. Many people know full well that they're being used by an unhappy and dissatisfied spouse that belongs to someone else, but they don't really care, because the sex is good and the conversation builds their self-esteem.

I've seen people walk down the aisle with a user, and knew they were marrying a user but did it anyway. Givers are willing to blind themselves to the obvious user motivations they see in people they're attracted to because they believe that they can help change them. People are willing to spend a lifetime of pain and abuse just for a little sexual attention. There would be a whole lot less users in our society if other people, and especially givers, put a demand of accountability on people who showed no sense of responsibility. Mothers who allow their grown sons to live with them scot free need to get tough and demand that they get a job and help pay for lodging. Parents who say that they didn't want to hurt their children's feelings need to understand that caring for a person's soul is more important than caring about their feelings. Feelings can and do change, but a person's soul can be damned and lost forever.

Fathers who become preoccupied with their work and fail to show their sons how to work are adding to the already great number of users. Users must encounter a heart change or else they'll die as users. Judas was a user. He wanted to do what was right but he was always over powered by the strong user spirit in his heart. He sought repentance but it was too late (). Imagine sitting and eating with the all-time greatest giver and not changing your heart attitude? Jesus knew that Judas was a user but He also knew that he a role to play in history (His-story). Now in your case as a giver you don't have to allow users to keep on using you and other people, but you can confront them boldly and maybe even help them change. People who are givers need help in understanding that predatory people will seek to use their generosity for their own self gain. Givers need help in overcoming the attraction to meeting everyone's need. We'll always have poor people among us, but givers need to examine the reasons why many people are poor. Are you poor by chance or by choice? The vast majority of people who start calling churches and other places of charity organizations every year around the first week of December are poor by choice. Why is it that some people only need money at Christmas time? These people will turn down food and clothes because they want you to give them cash money. They want cash money because they want to buy drugs or gamble with it. It's okay to give a man a fish as long as you show him how to catch fish for himself. All too often in our country the users get the goodies and the givers get got. Of course it's your fault if you keep on getting got after having been gotten for so long.

If a person is smart and crafty enough to know how to use the system, and other people as well, then he is able to work and make an honest living. It may not be the type of work you desire but at least you're working. You're putting your hands to something. You've humbled yourself and taken on the spirit of a child and are not thinking of yourself more higher than you ought to. Being a part of the solution to society's problems is greater than being the ongoing problem. People who love the Lord don't need to continue to aid and abet users by allowing them to giving the "freebies" all the time either.

Users prey on Church folk

The church is like a gigantic magnet that attracts users like salmon and rice attracts gnats. Oh how I loved it when my mother fixed salmon and rice. In the rural southwestern town of Monroeville, Alabama where I grew up we always found it very difficult to eat salmon and rice in the summer time because the gnats just wouldn't back off. We didn't have air conditioning, so the warm air was the perfect environment for gnats to fester in. It really didn't matter if we were inside or outside, the gnats would find the salmon and rice. There's an atmosphere in church that seems conducive to people who have ulterior motives. The good always seems to attract the bad. Is it because like charges repel and unlike charges attract? I know that the bible teaches us to be givers, but it never says that we have to be gullible.

The church's gullibility has even landed users behind the pulpit. When churches that are out of biblical order use search committees to find themselves a new pastor they leave the door wide open for the gnats (the user preachers) to come in. The succeeding leadership was never meant to come from without, but was to be raised up as it walked in the footsteps of the fathers who showed the way. Believe me; I hear your objection to what I'm saying: "What do you expect us to do; we have to have a pastor over the church?" Now right here is where you and your "churchy church" doctrine and the Word of God differ. The one man governmental system of "the pastor" cannot be found anywhere in the bible. Nor can you find in the bible where a board of deacons chooses the new pastor. Voting for the pastor is of the devil. Voting by secret ballot is an idea that came straight from the pits of hell. Users are attracted to systematic religion like the gnats were to my favorite dish of salmon and rice. Have you ever tried to fight gnats off? They're tiny insects that are very elusive and determined. You can kill a swarm of gnats but they seem to keep multiplying. It's very interesting that when the salmon and rice is gone and the dishes are all washed and clean that the gnats all disappear. But don't breathe so easy though, because they'll return in full force the very next time you have salmon and rice. Users, just like gnats, are drawn to smelly food stuff. The hot and humid climate is the perfect environment for them to reproduce in.

Users are always there even when you're not serving smelly food, but it's the combination of the heat and the aroma that brings them out. Users know exactly what smelly church folk want. People who reek with the smell of immaturity, preacheritis (the love of moaning and groaning), and disorder provide the perfect atmosphere for users to thrive. User preachers know exactly what people want. They know what to tune, how to tune, and when to tune. Tuning is real popular in certain denominations where people look forward to hearing it. I'm sorry, I forgot to tell you what tuning was. Tuning is what I call the musical style, high low, and moaning, groaning, special effects style of preaching. Now, I know that Jesus preached and taught people, but I really don't know what His style was. The style of preaching is not what we should focus on, but rather the motive of the one doing the preaching.

The user doesn't care about the people; all he wants is the money and the praise of how good he "sounded". Many user preachers started preaching because they had good singing voices. In fact, some men started preaching because somebody told them that they had a good and beautiful voice and that God had called them to preach. So they confessed their calling to preach, did their "trial" sermon, had a church assigned to them, and have been using since that time. I am very familiar with this type system because I came through form it. I confessed my calling, and I indeed was called of God (but so was everyone else), I preached my trial sermon, and was voted in as the pastor of the church. The fact that I survived the system doesn't make me or the system right. Since then I have learned better. I know that my heart and my motives are pure, and I have shunned men who want to use people. What I needed was not a church to pastor, but a spiritual father to honor and serve. I've seen young men with wives and children and the itch to preach, get a church, become lifted up in pride over their enormous gift, start stealing money from the church, committing adultery, and divorce their wives and lose everything.

Since these young men don't have spiritual fathers they become prime rib for many of the OGU's (Old Gangster Users).

These old gangster users can no longer tune like they use to, so they prey on the gifs and talents of young men who look up to them. These young men are used to bring more people to the church, which in turn means bigger offerings. Many of these young men are destroyed because they become lifted up in pride over the anointing and gifts they have. A young man that can preach the word of God and sing like a canary does not need the constant company of older preachers. If he's in high school he needs the company of his peers, or if he's in college he needs to be around his friends. Just because you're anointed doesn't mean that you must hang out with old preachers, neither does it mean that you have to stay home and read the bible all the time. People who do this will destroy themselves because there's no balance in their lives. It's really a dead end street because young men (women too) lay awake on their beds at night dreaming of the day when they will become pastor of the church, or a famous singer. God has already warned us that except He builds the house, or whatever it is we're trying to build, then all of our efforts are in vain (Psalms 127:1).

God is the Ultimate Giver-He's our Father

God's way is the way of giving. He gave us the earth and everything in it. He gave us houses and land and silver and gold. He gave us parents to nurture and train us. He gave us His Son and many exceeding great and precious promises. He has given us the bible, His holy Word so that we may know what to do. He gave us the Holy Spirit so that we would know the things that He freely gave us. He gave us the pattern of worship in the Old Testament Tabernacle of Moses. Have you ever studied it? Or do you just look at the New Testament and never realize that the New is in the old concealed, and that the Old is in the New revealed? The New is in the Old contained, and the Old is in the New explained. God gave us fathers in the old book because God Himself is the Father of all. God is a good Father in heaven and His will is that there be good fathers in the earth. Now since the fathers have eaten the sour grapes and have set the children's teeth on edge, fatherhood is no longer limited to biological offspring but has become spiritual as well.

The Father has given us A Son in Jesus, and the Son who is the express image of the Father, has given us an order, or pattern to follow. God has also given us time. But why has He given us time? We have been given time so that God can manifest all He has ever planned for us. What we're experiencing in time right now is the "groaning and travailing "of the earth as it awaits the manifestation of the "sons" of God (Romans 8: 22). The natural disasters such as tornadoes, hurricanes, tsunamis, earthquakes, floods, and cyclones are real to life destroyers, but they also speak symbolically of the destruction done in the lives of God's people by sin and disorder. Just take a look around you. Family life has been devastated. Mothers and grandmothers have to lead the home. Two women in a relationship are in the courts fighting for the right to be together and to raise children. Oh, don't get nervous or upset, women are only doing it because men have done it first. God gave us an order, or pattern, for life as well as for church, but we've allowed sin, lust, pride, and religious tradition to reign instead. Children need fathers.

The leadership of God as revealed in the bible was always "patriarchal" for the most part, but since the fathers have fallen asleep and "mother nature" has taken the reins, things are all messed up. Any woman in her right mind will gladly accept the leading of a good and godly man who leads by precept and example. There are women who will not accept what I just said, but remember I did say, "Any woman in her right mind". Chauvinism and feminism both find their death as well as their proper function in Christ. God gave us fathers (nurturers, caretakers, providers, protectors, and shepherds, lovers) to show us His way. People are so religiously confused over things that the bible speaks about in certain places. For example, the bible says that we are to "call no man father upon the earth", but it never meant that men were not to "function" as fathers, because that's exactly what God the heavenly Father wants men to do. A man must learn to function as a father, and never demand that people call him father. Being a good father is more important than just doing the deeds of a father. God's anointing rests upon the man as he fearfully performs his function as a father. Remember, Abram means "like a father", but Abraham means "father of many nations". So who then is our father, God or Abraham?

Jesus makes it clear to those Jews who called Abraham their father that before Abraham was ever born, He was (John 8). If these religious Jews had been behaving like children of Abraham, Jesus would have never rebuked them for acting like their true father, the devil. When you honor a man in the earth who functions as a father you likewise honor your Father in heaven. Fathers give. They give life to people. They sire and sustain. They nurture and help bring to maturity to those connected to them. They also circumcise, or cut away things that can cause life to be destroyed or hindered. The pastor of the church may or may not be true father. If he is a hireling then he is not a true father. I have a true spiritual father, Dr. Mark Hanby, who does not pastor a local church, but he indeed does function as a father of the message that says God is turning the hearts of fathers to children and the hearts of children to their fathers, or else the book entitled "You Have Not Many Fathers" is one that I highly recommend you read. Men who are users have taken Dr. earth will be smitten with a curse (Malachi 4:4-6). Dr.Hanby has written many books, but his Hanby's book and used it as a basis for collecting the tithe. The bible does teach that sons should honor fathers.

The word honor in the Greek has the meaning of value, money paid, or esteem of the highest degree. We should certainly want to give honor to whom honor is due, and not just in word only, but also with our riches as well. Many men in the ministry of the Lord Jesus give riches to men they've received as spiritual fathers on a regular basis. I have always honored my spiritual father with riches on a monthly basis for as long as I have received him as my spiritual father. The tithe was always heaved up by the high priest. So now when we give honor to a spiritual father we are really recognizing and acknowledging that Jesus Christ is our High Priest after the order of Melchizedek, the earthly King of Salem to whom Abraham gave tithes of all that he had

Chapter Eleven
Who called you to Preach?
Who's Your Daddy?

J esus didn't call Himself to preach; He followed the order of God for ministry (the order of father and son) as God had already established (Hebrews 5:5). You can read Jesus' genealogy, or lineage, for yourself because it's recorded in the gospels. We know where He came from and who He came through. He did not call Himself to preach! Today, men do whatever they feel like doing as they announce their own calling, get them a church, and take the tithe from the congregation, but they themselves will give honor to no one. Really, the members of the church have no basis to give their tithe if there is no priest over the house that tithes up to Jesus by giving tithe (honor) to an earthly spiritual father. Men will argue with this and say,

"I don't like that, that's not bible!" Well, you're totally without understanding at this point, but hang in there and get more Word in you, because when you get enough Word in you you'll see it immediately and lead the way for others. Stop beating the people you pastor over the head with Malachi 3:8, because this scripture wasn't written to the saints, but to selfish and prideful preachers. There's a lot of misuse and abuse concerning spiritual fathering so let me just say a few things about it right here.

A spiritual father is not a boss who follows you around to see if you're doing everything correct. He is not someone who tells you how to run the church you oversee. The vision for your ministry comes from God- not from your spiritual father, nor from the denominational headquarters. A spiritual father is a divinely appointed connection in God that must always honor God Himself. Why do you think that the gospel writers go to the trouble to list a genealogy for the Lord Jesus Christ? It's because in the bible if you wanted to be a priest (preacher) you had to be the son of a priest. In other words, "who is your daddy?" It's sad, but today preachers can tell you what denominational organization they belong to, and even what bible school they graduated from, but cannot name a spiritual father. Now please don't panic because you have never honored a spiritual father. The system you're in was messed up when you joined it, and unless men begin to search matters out, it'll probably stay that way. So don't run off looking for a spiritual father because you'll find the wrong one.

Spiritual DNA

No one can tell you who your spiritual father is, in the same way that no one, including you, can decide who your biological father is. DNA tests verify who the real father of a child is. If

DNA tests can prove the truth in the physical or natural realm, then how much more can the Holy Ghost let us know who our father in the spirit is? Some men are searching for their spiritual father the way people go shopping for a new automobile. This one is too high, that one is too old, I don't like the color of that one, I can't afford that one, this one burns too much gas, and that one's not popular enough. The order of father and son is as real as the bible is the Word of God, but there will always be men with impure motives who will prey upon the simple minded and the gullible. There are users out there who are just waiting for you to find them. The true voice of the heavenly Father is what connects us to the divine flow of revelation truth that flows from His throne. When Elisabeth heard the greeting of Mary the babe inside her womb (John the Baptist) leaped, and she was filled with the Holy Ghost.

You may have a thousand instructors and tutors in your life but you'll only have one father who speaks and connects you to your purpose and destiny. Timothy had Lois and Eunice in his life but it was Paul who took him and imparted the spiritual DNA of God into his life. It's like this, a woman can have sex with five or six men but only one of them will be the biological father. My life has never been the same since 1998 when I heard the voice of my heavenly father connecting me to my eternal purpose and destiny as Dr. Mark Hanby spoke. Now I know that many will object to what I've said and exclaim, "I can hear from God for myself!" That is exactly right, so why can't you hear the truth of what I've said? And if God is your Father why don't you honor Him? I know why you won't hear it. It's because you're a user, and you refuse to come into proper order and alignment. You haven't become a kingdomgarten kid-you're grown up in years but you're a toddler in your understanding. You honor no one but yourself. You may pastor a church of multiple thousands but you'll eventually die with multitudes at your funeral, but you won't have one true son to continue the vision that you say God gave you fifty years ago. When you die the vision will die with you, and the church will hire a stranger to come in and start all over again. During all of your years in ministry you gave honor to no one as a father, and now there will be not one son to honor you in your golden years. Users use up everything and their offspring and their followers inherit poverty.

The world's economy is at an all-time low today because of the "user" mentality. If a giver dies and leaves his wealth in the hands of a user son, the cycle of poverty just starts all over again. Ghetto life, slum life, and trailer- park trash life exist in the church and are all created by users. Children didn't ask to be born into poverty, but many indeed are because their parents probably were born into it also but never did anything to improve their quality of life. If you're crossing a lake in a boat with a small hole in it and all you do is sit there and watch the water fill the boat, then what you need is a bar of soap so that you can at least die smelling good. Good men, and men who have learned how to give, leave an inheritance for their children's children. Oh if users had only learned to share in kingdomgarten then life wouldn't be so hard for them today.

Chapter Twelve
The King of Non- Violence

Violence has completely permeated our world. The need for safety is at an all-time high. According to Abraham Maslow, a famous psychologist, the need for a safe environment and protection from harm, is one of man's basic needs. In other words after we get food, water, and air, our next need is that of a safe environment. Well, as we speak the food and water we use are no longer as safe to consume as they once were, the air we breathe is highly contaminated, and the environment we live in is definitely a dangerous one. There's violence in the home, in the workplace, at school, in churches, at vacation spots, in the air, at sea, and even beneath the earth's surface. Most small children consume a steady supply of violent images every day. If it's not live in the home where they live, then it's on television, in the neighborhood streets, or on screen at the theater.

The images of fighting, murder, kidnapping, high jacking, terrorism, flooding, and destructive natural forces are all that many people ever see. I won't bore you with statistics on violence because I want to make better use of paper space, however if you're interested in statistical data you can log on To the "WHO" (World Health Organization) website at www.thepeacealliance. org and see all the stats you desire to see. I can tell you that the numbers will stagger you, and in some cases maybe they won't as such a large segment of our population has been nearly desensitized by the constant flow of violence in our world. Many people have had to learn violence as a way of survival. Others have had to resort to violent measures in order to protect themselves, their loved ones, and their property. People who have never owned guns are now gun owners. Weapons are so readily available and accessible. When you connect the accessibility of weapons with the inability of modern day youth to resolve problems and conflict, violence and death are usually the result.

Dr. Martin Luther King Jr. gave his life in an attempt to show the world how to solve problems in a non-violent manner. His efforts were not just so that African American people could have equal treatment under the law but so that all people could have the same opportunities for life, liberty, and the pursuit of happiness. Nelson Mandela, in his foreword for the first World Report on Violence and Health, said this: "We owe our children—the most vulnerable citizens in our society—a life free from violence and fear. In order to ensure this, we must be tireless in our efforts not only to attain peace, justice and prosperity for countries, but also for communities and members of the same family. We must address the roots of violence. Only then will we transform the past century's legacy from a crushing burden into a cautionary lesson." If we're going to address the "roots of violence" then we have to start with the intrinsic nature of man. All men are born into this world with the potential to become mass murderers, serial killers, rapists, terrorists, drug dealers, and anything else you can name. All men are also born with the potential to do well and to become productive members of society.

Man was created to be fruitful and to multiply, and to replenish the earth. When man sinned, or rebelled against God's authority, man became a "lawless" individual. Lawlessness and violence are very closely connected. Sin is lawlessness, and lawlessness is the overturning of God's authority. Lucifer became the devil when he was booted out of heaven for trying to be God himself, and he then afterwards introduces the spirit of rebellion and lawlessness in the earth. This spirit is in Adam and Eve, and it is also in their children. No sooner than Cain is faced with a conflict he resorts to violence and kills his own brother. Cain wasn't raised in a violent environment but he still murdered his brother. Today we now know that all violent individuals don't necessarily have to have come from violent surroundings. Violence may fill your community, but it's only there because it's really inside of the violent individual. Because of sin we all live in a violent world. The spirit of violence is the same today as it was in Noah's day; it's just that there are more violent crimes being committed today for the obvious reason that there are more people on the planet. Many people like to sit around and talk about how safe it was years ago to leave your doors unlocked or your keys in your car and nobody bothered anything, but what they fail to realize is that that happened in their community and the same thing wasn't true for every community everywhere, because somewhere somebody in some location was being robbed or killed. It tends not to be real if it's not happening in our neck of the woods.

The King and His Kingdom

Since violence is deeply rooted in sin, what are we to do? We need to recognize that Jesus is the King of non-violence. Jesus was a Jew, and the Jewish people have a history of violence. If you don't believe this then you've never read your bible. Jesus' lineage can be traced through Abraham, and Abraham is a descendent of Shem, one of Noah's three sons. Noah only had three sons, and the entire present day world population descends from one of the three sons of Noah. So that means that all of mankind is somehow related. The Arabic people are also descendents of Abraham by his son Ishmael. God said that Ishmael would be a wild man; his hand would be against every man, and every man's hand against him; and that he would dwell in the presence of all his brethren (Genesis 16:12). Let us not be fooled to believe that the Middle East is the capital of violence; for that would be a mistake. The Germans, the Russians, Orientals, Latinos, Indians, Africans, Whites, and Blacks all have their share of violent people. The whole world das violent people because all people are born in sin and shaped in iniquity. Only when men turn to Jesus is the violence slowed, not stopped, but slowed. When men refuse to yield to Jesus the violence may even escalate. God visits the sins of fathers upon children to the third, and even the fourth generation. Abraham wasn't a murderer, a liar maybe, his son Isaac wasn't a murderer (a liar also), Jacob wasn't a murderer either (definitely a deceiver), but now Jacob has twelve boys and a few of them will surely commit violent acts. These are Jesus' kinfolk I'm talking about. IF you think that Jesus didn't know what kind of people his relatives were you're short enough to walk under the crack between the bottom of the door and the floor. He knows what's in every one of us. HE knew that Peter would cut the servant's ear off, but He miraculously put it back on because He wants every man to hear His voice and turn from violence.

Those who live by the sword will die by the sword. The Romans were very violent people, and Jesus' disciples, who were Jews, wanted Him to start a revolution against the Romans. The disciples were very disappointed when they discovered that Jesus' plan was to die on a wooden cross, but it will not be the violent Romans who insist that Jesus die; it will be His own kin folk who order His death. In John chapter eighteen as Jesus is standing in the midst of violent men He makes a statement that should cause us all to dig deeper: "My kingdom is not of this world: If my kingdom were of this world, then would my servants fight, that I should not be delivered to the Jews (His own people): But now is my kingdom not from hence" (John 18:36). Our only hope in this life of escaping violence and all other evils as well is to see the kingdom that is not from here, and no one can see it unless they become "as" a little child. Violence floods our world because of sinful men who don't "see" things eye to eye, and men don't see eye to eye because they don't see the kingdom that Jesus spoke of. Whether it's two countries fighting, two states fighting, two cities fighting, two communities fighting, two families fighting, two churches fighting, two gangs fighting, or two people fighting—the reason is pretty much the same: there has been a failure to see His kingdom and submit to the King's rule.

The church, the called out ones, is made up of every ethnic group or culture that there is on the earth. God's plan is to introduce us to an entirely new kingdom culture and make us citizens of it. The world has never seen the kingdom of God culture because the church is busy fighting personal wars. Every reason or issue that causes men to become violent and fight can be categorized into one of three reasons: The lust of the flesh, the lust of the eyes and the pride of life; these three things summarize everything that there is in the entire world (1 John 2:16). The world that the writer is referring to is not the terra firma but the system of ideas that oppose God; it's the antichrist, or mindset that opposes the will of God. The antichrist is not a man, who lives in the Middle East, but he's the man, or mindset, that lives in your middle, or in the middle between your two ears. People are so spooked about the anti-Christ until they've started naming certain world leaders the anti-Christ. I received e-mails from people who were so shook up over the fact that Barack Obama was going to be America's first black president that they were finding information that proved he was indeed the anti-Christ. The bible never uses the definite article "the" in none of the five references of the term "antichrist". Antichrist is the spirit that denies that Jesus is the Christ, and that God lives in man's flesh. Antichrist is a lying spirit that denies the Father and the Son. Jesus wasn't one of the prophets; He wasn't just a good teacher, for He is the Christ, the Son of the living God. Antichrist denies the Fatherhood of God, and this is the reason that so many Christians won't become kingdomgarten kids. God is a loving Father who cares for all of His kids, but when people make Him some stiff, grim-faced mean old man sitting on a throne, the wrong impression of who He is has been presented. There are also good and godly earthly fathers present in the world today, but if you have the wrong impression of your heavenly Father (in your flesh) then you'll probably reject your father in the spirit as well. If you don't see things from God's perspective you'll always fight against Him. Just as small children trust their fathers to take care of them, likewise Christians must also learn to trust God the Father to take care of them.

Christians must be vigilant and not violent. We are to never take matters into our own hands as the "vigilantes" did in the old westerns we used to watch on television whenever they thought that the bad guys would not be punished sufficiently by the law. We are however are to be "vigilant", watchful, or responsible, and arm ourselves with the armor of righteousness which allows God to bring all disobedience to its knees. God our heavenly Father is ready to revenge all disobedience as soon as ours is fulfilled (2 Corinthians 10:6). Christians are never to be violent towards the lives and liberties of other people but rather be violent in their attitude towards attitudes and mind sets that come against their pursuit of the kingdom of God. The violent take the kingdom by force, or we crush and kill any and every spirit that attempts to hinder us as we advance the kingdom. Our weapons are not carnal but they are mighty through God to the pulling down (now that's violent) of strongholds, casting down imaginations, and every high thing that exalts itself against the knowledge of God, and makes every thought (anti-christed ideas) obedient to God. We haven't done anything until we've become violent with our own crazy minds and surrendered them to the King of our non- violent kingdom. The reason why so much moral decay, sexual perversion, lack of accountability, and divorce exist in the church today is simply because we've not become violent enough to destroy the spirit that plant these thoughts in our mind. If all you ever do is sit around and talk about how bad and dirty somebody's sin is, then you're destined to do the same type sins, but only worse. Christians who don't submit themselves to the King of non-violence will continue to go round and round in circles all lifelong. They will be forever learning "stuff" but will never come to a full knowledge of spiritual truth that actually puts them over into a new way of life.

Many have already died going through the ritual of what they call "having church". They died hating someone because of the color of their skin, or because they didn't worship God on Sunday, or even worse because they sang songs that weren't southern gospel, or black gospel songs. What's black or southern about the gospel? Absolutely nothing, but in our utter insanity we've created stuff that continues to divide us more and more. The idea of a "black" or "white" church is absolutely asinine. The bible never refers to church as black, white, Baptist, Methodist, catholic, Pentecostal, holiness, Presbyterian, or with any other adjective or noun. The church belongs to Christ and is called "His church", or the household of God. We carry this type foolishness on because we lost our identity in the garden and refuse to see His kingdom and become "as" little children.

Epilogue
Whole lotta Shaking Going On

Jerry Lee Lewis had a very popular song in 1957 entitled, "Whole Lotta Shaking Going On". In his song Jerry Lee was inviting "Baby" to come on over to his place and join in on all the shaking that was going on. In the song Jerry Lee promises Baby that she couldn't go wrong by coming on over. Jerry Lee Lewis was a very hard-working and passionate singer/musician who encouraged his audiences to sing and shake right along with him. Well, I don't know if you're into shaking or not but it'll probably help if you are because there's certainly a whole lotta shaking going on. No, It doesn't matter if you got an invitation or not, because the shaking is coming to your neighborhood, and even to your house. There's a whole lotta shaking going on. According to the writer of the book of Hebrews everything that can be shaken will be shaken so that those things which cannot be shaken may remain (Hebrews 12:27-29).

The term "shaken" comes from the Greek word *saleuo*, which means a motion produced by winds, storms, and waves. It implies agitation, tottering, or shaking together. Furthermore it means to shake down (like the policemen do with crooks), or overthrow; it means to cast down from one's happy and secure state, to agitate the mind, or to disturb. When I first looked at this word I thought about the times that I've gone deep sea fishing. I love deep sea fishing, and I'm never really bothered by the back and forth motion of the sea, but for many people the drama, or shaking, of the sea cause severe nausea and vomiting. In fact, I've seen many who went deep sea fishing actually end up "deep sea feeding", if you know what I mean. I've even seen cases where the patch and Dramamine didn't even help, as helpless fishermen spent their entire fishing excursion with their heads over the side of the boat.

Children love to shake, rattle and roll

Do you remember when you were a small child? You could go round and round, up and down, and it never bothered you. You went to Six Flags and rode everything in the park twice, but these days you go to the park and sleep in the car the entire time. You just don't like a lot of motion, or shaking. Well, you may as well get you a full supply of spiritual Dramamine because the shake is on, and everything that can be shaken will be shaken. The heavens, the earth, the nations, the church, the government, the economy, the home, the family, and marriages are all being shaken. There's a whole lotta shaking going on- isn't it?

In lieu of all the shaking going on the best thing for Christians to do is to become "as little children" and enjoy the ride. Oh yeah, I know that you're praying for all the shaking to stop, but it's not going to stop until the church comes into order and alignment. Stop pretending you don't know what I'm talking about, for you know what it's like to drive your car when it needs a front end alignment and new shocks. You've worn out three sets of new tires already, and until you get that front end properly aligned you're going to wear out plenty more tires Look at you, driving your car down the street and fussing like crazy because it's shaking like a leaf on a tree, but you insist upon driving it in the shape it's in anyway. You're stubborn as a mule because you refuse to change your mind about the situation with your car. Well, I've got news for you, God is not about to change His mind about His glorious kingdom either. His kingdom has come, and His will shall be done with or without you. Unfortunately, many people will miss out on all the great things that could have been in this life because they never became kingdomgarten kids.

Throughout this book I've tried to emphasize how important foundations are. Everything you accomplish in life will be determined by how good your foundations are. Regardless of your cultural background there are certain foundational principles that are basic and relevant to all people. Food, water, and air are basic to all humans. A man also has to provide shelter and safety for himself and his family. Work is not an option for man; he must either work for himself or for someone else. If a man refuses to work then he should not eat. Men must also show respect for each other's persons and property. A high value must be placed upon all life. Children must be taught to accept responsibility for their actions. As I attempt to bring closure to Kingdomgarten Kids, I'd like to encourage you to take heart as you look at all the chaos that exists around you, for God is faithful to complete the work He started in you long before you ever knew who you were. God is shaking everything at its foundation because that's where we're hurting. Our foundations are all messed up. Christ is the one and only true foundation. He is the rock upon which the wise man built his house and the winds and rain could not destroy it. Christ cannot be destroyed.

The carnal mind, or the gates of hell, cannot prevail against His church. The Psalmist asks a question in Psalms 11:3 that says if the foundation is destroyed what can the righteous do? The answer is that the righteous won't have to worry about doing anything because Christ, who is our foundation, cannot be destroyed, and the foundation of God stands sure, having this seal, the Lord knows them that are His. The foundation of the fake, or harlot, church is religious traditions of men. The foundation of the true church, the one that Jesus is building, is the apostles and prophets, and Jesus Christ Himself the chief cornerstone. I believe that the reason or at least one of the reasons, that God is shaking everything at its foundation is because He wants every soul in His church to "fall on the Rock and be broken, rather than have the Rock fall on them and they be crushed to powder (Matthew 21:44). The tiny little kingdoms of our selfish pursuits must become the kingdom of our Lord and of His Christ. As gorgeous as our kingdoms or ourselves may look, they must be broken so that the greater glory of God's kingdom may appear. Christians must become Disciples of Christ and not disciples of men and religions. If we're to be spoiled then let us be spoiled after Christ, the truth, and not after theories. Men have built many kingdoms down through the ages, but where are the kingdomgarten kids? David wanted to build something good looking for God, but God said "no" to him, and He's said the same thing to us today, but we still insist upon doing it anyway.

There's no salvation in any denomination (Baptist, Methodist, Pentecostal, etc.) or historical figure (Abraham, Moses, Mohammed, the Virgin Mary, Paul, etc.) we choose to conjure up. Salvation is in Christ and Him alone. The problem in our world is that many people believe in Jesus but they always stop short of the promise of entering His rest (Hebrews 4:1). You see, as long as people can keep working for God, or doing their own thing, they're perfectly happy, but once you tell them that God is at rest and that they have to stop working for Him and enter His rest where everything is already finished, they immediately become offended. If after walking with the Lord for so long you can still be offended, then it only proves that you don't love His law as you should (Psalms 119: 165). As you look upon the world's situation are you optimistic? Are you hopeful? Have you been shook up? Are you offended? Well I'd like to close by offering you an opportunity to rest a spell. Yes, I recommend naptime! In public schools they cut naptime out after kindergarten, but perhaps it wouldn't be a bad idea for the rest of the grades also. Oh yes, there's always one or two small children who don't want to take a nap, but I think that they are symbolic of the many Christians who to rest in the Lord, and ultimately they'll wear themselves out worry and anxiety. For those who argue with this and say that we need to hurry up because we don't have that much time left, I say that they need to take a deep breath and exhale real slow, because they're right, we don't have much time left, in fact we're already out of time and into eternity with Christ seated at the right hand of the Father in heavenly places. All we're doing on earth is declaring from our exalted position in Christ at the Father's right hand, "thy will be done, in earth, as it has already been done in heaven." Amen

Acknowledgements

I'm thankful to God for His marvelous grace that has allowed me to finish this book in spite of my own procrastination. I am eternally grateful to my wife Jackie, my two sons Duane and Charles, and my daughter in-law Reghan for their confidence in me to go ahead and finish this book. To Henry and Elvira McPherson, my parents, thank you for teaching me to be tolerant of all people as I grew up in rural south Alabama during a very confusing time in history. To my deceased in-laws, Samuel and Ruby Turner, thank you for producing a wonderful daughter in Jackie, who became my wife and my number one fan. To members of the church that I'm blessed to oversee, thanks for always asking me where I was in completing the book. To Dr. Mark Hanby, thanks for providing me with a real live picture of someone who is super serious about the kingdom of God, but knows how to relax and have fun with people. Thanks to Victor Isaacs Jr. for designing the front cover. Thanks to Elder Stan Cash for assisting me with the technical aspects of submitting the manuscript to the publisher. And to a myriad of friends and acquaintances I've made down through the years that have left lasting impressions in my mind-thank you for the special touches of inspiration.

www.ingramcontent.com/pod-product-compliance
Lightning Source LLC
Chambersburg PA
CBHW051210120626
46547CB00013B/1286